BASICS

TYPOGRAPHY

01   Virt

Matthias Hillner

ava | Academia
the environment of learning

An AVA Book
Published by AVA Publishing SA
Rue des Fontenailles 16
Case Postale
1000 Lausanne 6
Switzerland
Tel: +41 786 005 109
Email: enquiries@avabooks.ch

Distributed by Thames & Hudson (ex-North America)
181a High Holborn
London WC1V 7QX
United Kingdom
Tel: +44 20 7845 5000
Fax: +44 20 7845 5055
Email: sales@thameshudson.co.uk
www.thamesandhudson.com

Distributed in the USA & Canada by
Ingram Publisher Services Inc.
1 Ingram Blvd.
La Vergne, TN 37086
USA
Tel: +1 866 400 5351
Fax: +1 800 838 1149
Email:
customer.service@ingrampublisherservices.com

English Language Support Office
AVA Publishing (UK) Ltd.
Tel: +44 1903 204 455
Email: enquiries@avabooks.ch

ISBN 2-940373-99-X and 978-2-940373-99-4

10 9 8 7 6 5 4 3 2 1

Design by Create/Reject

Production by AVA Book Production Pte. Ltd., Singapore
Tel: +65 6334 8173
Fax: +65 6259 9830
Email: production@avabooks.com.sg

All reasonable attempts have been made to trace, clear and credit the
copyright holders of the images reproduced in this book. However,
if any credits have been inadvertently omitted, the publisher will
endeavour to incorporate amendments in future editions.

Contents

This book introduces different aspects of virtual typography, via dedicated chapters for each topic. Each chapter provides numerous examples of work by leading designers, annotated to explain the reasons behind the design choices made. The examples shown include a range of screen-resolution works and diagrams, which, when combined with detailed analysis in the text, create a fascinating insight into the world of virtual typography.

Section header
Each chapter is broken down into sub-sections, the title of which can be found in the top left corner of each spread.

Image caption
Image captions provide in-depth information about the images shown.

2.2   Temporal and transitional typography   40—41

Unfolded – Tomi Vollauschek
Tomi Vollauschek, who co-founded the London-based design agency FL@33 in London in 2001, created this animated typeface in 1999 when he studied at the Royal College of Art in London. The type evolves from diamond-shaped graphic elements which virtually unfold into squares, then into lines, and finally into letter shapes. The end result is a simple pixel font. But the transition, which is accompanied by a subtle flapping sound, lends the typeface an entertaining, humorous quality. Vollauschek's AAT (acoustic animated typeface) application, which includes an animated display of Unfolded, can be downloaded for free from the FL@33 website <www.flat33.com>.

Temporal typography is a term that can be used synonymously with transitional typography to characterise typographic forms which change dynamically over time. Changes in type size, weight and position can be used in order to enhance the expressiveness of typographic messages. It is important to note that temporal or time-based typography does not accelerate the process of reading: it usually slows it down. But we may ask ourselves if it is at all beneficial to read at a fast pace. If we can argue that the pace of reading relates to the reader's memorisation of text, then we may assume that reading at a slow pace makes text information more memorable. One of the key advantages of transitional typography is that emotive expression can be enhanced by the definition of the graphic transition. A word written with a fairly standard-looking font can become expressive due to the way it changes over time.

'Only that which is absent can be imagined.'
Marcel Proust

Chapter footers
This shows the current chapter and sub-section, and also shows past and future sub-sections.

Virtual Typography

Running glossary
Clarification and explanation of key terms is provided alongside the main text.

How do you define a journey? – Adam Field
Adam Field was a student at the London College of Communication when he created this large-format print. Field hoped to break down words to allow for multiple interpretations of his typographic composition. The type communicates on two layers: the question appears from the omission of type in certain areas and becomes increasingly illegible towards the end, yet the seemingly random letters surrounding the letters that shape the question invite the reader to search for words within the chaos of the type. While the words, which evolve from the gaps between letters, phrase the question, the form of their visual presentation point towards an answer. A journey through text defined by chance?

Edmund Husserl

In the context of philosophy Edmund Husserl (1859–1938) is seen as the founder of phenomenology, a branch of philosophy that considers all knowledge to be rooted in people's subjective experience. Many other philosophers including Heidegger, Merleau-Ponty, Sartre and Derrida drew on Husserl's theories. Husserl taught philosophy at various universities in Germany until he retired in Freiburg, where he was superseded by Martin Heidegger in 1928.

Time and tension

As much as one sentence points to the next to come, it also relates to the expectation triggered by the previous one. By fulfilling or contradicting the expectations made, each sentence modifies the understanding of what was previously said. So the text is constantly re-evaluated and the reader's memories transformed. In a wider sense, this process of continuously rethinking the past and the future reflects the way people perceive temporal progression in general. According to **Edmund Husserl**, a German philosopher, the present moment can only be perceived indirectly through the dialectical tension between past and future events. In other words, people develop their awareness of the present through constantly comparing their expectations of what is about to happen in the future to that which has happened. Husserl refers to the anticipation of future events as 'protensions' and to memorised sensations as 'retentions'. Like the present moment in real life, the content of a written text remains constantly dynamic. Depending on the sequential structure of sentences and contents, new thoughts are evoked and the reader's perspective is shifted. The continual interplay between protensions and retentions can result in a constantly upheld tension. Following Iser, protensions in the context of literature should therefore not lead to fulfillment, but to a succession of protensions. This allows for the constantly upheld tension that sustains the reader's interest and perpetuates the joy of reading.

'Faced with the beautiful, analytical reflection restores the temps durée through the medium of its antithesis. Analysis terminates in beauty.'
Theodor Adorno

⊕ Typography and the process of reading: 5.4 The prospective interpretation of text contents
5.3 Saccadic eye movements ← → 5.5 Time consciousness

Quotes
Additional quotes from subject experts and practitioners.

Graphic design is a means of visual communication, but only one of many: people also communicate through gestures, facial expression, body posture, images and written words. Animals also communicate through gestures, facial expression, body posture and images, but without words. Words constitute verbal language, which is exclusive to mankind. The colourful striped pattern of a bee or a snake signalises danger and such image patterns constitute graphic signs which are capable of conveying more or less basic messages. But the flexibility of graphic or ideogrammatic systems is always limited to the number of signs available. The messages we exchange within human societies can be very complex, so they require more sophisticated means: words and writing.

Verbal languages consist of words and letters, the orderly arrangement of which allows for an infinite number of meanings. Civilised societies would probably have never developed without written languages. Without words, life in a civilised world would be too difficult to organise. In ancient times and during the medieval period, reading and writing was reserved for the leadership of societies so iconic imagery was used to communicate religious and political issues to illiterate people where required. But following Johannes Gutenberg's introduction of movable type, text has increasingly replaced images. This has spread over the course of the last 500 years, thus spreading knowledge and understanding throughout society, in particular since public education was established throughout most of Europe and America in the nineteenth century.

At present, a reversal of this process appears to be taking place. Over the course of the twentieth century, people's lives have become so interlinked and information so accessible, that we struggle to put up with the infinite amount of information with which we are confronted every day. The exchange of information that once enabled us to enhance social interaction is now often seen as a burden. The growing information overload has led to a change in the use of language. Where there is no time left for reading, we return to the use of images as substitutes for words.

Images can be perceived at a glance. Traffic signs, for example, provide mostly ideogrammatic information as discussed in *The Fundamentals of Typography* (Ambrose and Harris, 2006). A red circle with a horizontal white bar is perceived much more quickly than the words 'do not enter' and its perception does not depend on the information recipient's individual language background. Texts need to be read, and reading is an analytical and therefore time-consuming activity. But even if images can be perceived quickly, how swiftly are they understood? Meaning conveyed through images is usually less explicit than that which is delivered through words. Traffic signs are comparatively easy to interpret. A cross, on the other hand, can vary in meaning depending on the context. The word 'Christianity' offers more precision in semiotic terms than the abstract image of a 'cross'. So do the words 'plus', 'death', 'first aid' and so on. Images are always subject to the viewer's interpretation. The more complex an image is, the more room there is for interpretation and potential misinterpretation. People say a picture is worth a thousand words, but it is as if these thousands of words are all spoken simultaneously without any particular structure involved. Grammar rules force a speaker, a writer or a typographer to articulate words in a structured manner. This is why text communicates meaning with more precision than images.

So we still need to use text information where we want to avoid the misinterpretation of our message. Typography can be understood as the visual interpretation of verbal language. But how do we best communicate typographic information in a world of images? Virtual typography is time-based. Thus it operates on the borderline between image and text.

It attracts the viewer's attention due to its image-like appearance before developing into a written message. Virtual typography is consequently not simply a matter of extruding conventional fonts, letting type bounce across the screen or making it spin randomly within three dimensions. It is about producing sensible solutions for conveying text messages gradually and effectively within media environments. Typography is the visual arrangement of words and letters. Where such arrangements are time-based, the conventions we have in place for judging static typography are no longer sufficient. New principles apply.

1 From visual poetry to modern typography

Before assessing contemporary time-based typography, we need to deepen our understanding of the modern achievements in printed typography. This first chapter shows how the pioneers of modern typography broke with typographic conventions in the past in order to create typographic compositions which were (and possibly still are) ahead of their time.

2 Approaching multimedia

This chapter provides an overview of recent concepts of multimedia typography. It will enable us to develop a conceptual understanding of the role of time and space in the context of virtual typography. In response to the emergence of new expressions, this chapter also helps to avoid terminological misunderstandings.

3 Typography, information and communication

With the help of a range of case studies, this chapter explains some of the fundamental principles behind typographic communication in general and behind virtual typography in particular. Step by step, we establish a theoretical basis for the time-based communication of typographic information.

4 Digital typography

Following the invention of movable type and early
twentieth century avant-garde art movements,
the introduction of digital media was probably the
most radical change in the context of typographic
communication. This critical review of celebrated
designs puts digital typography into perspective.
It also highlights how quickly the digital revolution
ran out of steam.

5 Typography and the process of reading

Typographic communication cannot be understood
without understanding the process of reading.
This chapter explains a number of existing concepts
concerning the visual and intellectual perception of
text. Understanding reading as a time-based process
provides a better understanding of the benefits of
virtual typography.

6 The significance of ambiguity

This final chapter sums up and explains the aesthetic
principles of virtual typography. A wide range of
examples illustrate how virtual typography can be
used to enhance the communication process.

It must be acknowledged that this book addresses a
fundamentally new way of typographic communication.
Some of the scientific and philosophical principles which
led to its rationale are still subject to speculation. The
book may well be just one first step into a new form of
visual expression.

Typography is the visual representation of text information. One could argue that every typographic arrangement constitutes the image of a text, however abstract this image may be. Johannes Gutenberg's method of printing with movable type in the fifteenth century reinforced the convention of writing in straight lines, from top left to bottom right. It was not until the turn of the nineteenth century that artists began to rebel against those rules. Alongside the likes of Christian Morgenstern and Stéphane Mallarmé, Guillaume Apollinaire introduced the revolutionary idea of visualising poetic writing. This attempt to fuse text and image into visually challenging typographic compositions inspired many forms of typographic art, including futurism, Dadaism and even constructivism.

Eulogy for HNW – Joshua Reichert
Joshua Reichert, a renowned German printer and typographer, created this printed piece of typography as a tribute to the famous Dutch printer Hendrik Nicolaas Werkman, who inspired Reichert's experimental typography.

Guillaume Apollinaire

Guillaume Apollinaire was part of the artistic community of Montparnasse in Paris, France, to which Pablo Picasso, André Breton and Marcel Duchamp also belonged. Apollinaire is mainly known for his avant-garde poetry and he is credited for coining the term 'surrealism'.

Ferdinand de Saussure

Ferdinand de Saussure, a Swiss-born linguist, provided a foundation stone to linguistic philosophy with his seminal book *Course in General Linguistics* in 1916. His approach differed from earlier contemporaries' because it focussed on language in any one time and place rather than language in one place developing over time. He viewed language as a system of words and signs and as such proposed that the specific language spoken by someone directly affected their conscious awareness of the world. The significance of verbal language in the context of human perception remains an important subject of investigation.

Visual poetry broke with the conventions of traditional typography well before modern and postmodern forms of typography emerged. The beginnings of the movement are usually attributed to the early twentieth century even though there are much earlier examples of pictorial representation of texts. Visual poets returned to the use of pencil and paper in protest against the mechanisation of reading. The mechanical characteristics of reading are closely related to the mechanisation of writing. Despite the fact that **Guillaume Apollinaire** commissioned letterpress artists to print his poems, he initially drew them by hand. As they were composed without any technological constraints Apollinaire's ideograms escaped the conventions of linear writing and forced readers into a perceptual struggle. A visual poem confronts the reader with an initially confusing piece of information. One cannot tell if one is looking at an image-like text or at a text-like image. Visual poetry thus undermines **Ferdinand de Saussure**'s early twentieth-century theory of a structural relationship between people's mental concept of an object (image) and the word used to name the object (linguistic sign). In contrast, according to Saussure, the word constitutes the second-order **semiological system**, the image of an object constitutes the first-order semiological system. Visual poetry reverses this relationship by translating the written word back into an image. The written word here becomes the first-order signifying system, and the image becomes the second-order signifying system. This is why we may consider visual poetry as a truly revolutionary step in the context of visual communication.

'A structure becomes architectural, and not sculptural, when its elements no longer have their justification in nature.'
Guillaume Apollinaire

Semiological system

According to Saussure, a sign consists of a 'signifier' and a 'signified'. The image of an object, which we have in mind in connotation with the object itself, constitutes the first-order signifying system. The word that we attribute to the object in connotation with the image of the object constitutes the second-order signifying system.

IL PLEUT

Il pleut – Guillaume Apollinaire

Il pleut is one of Apollinaire's best-known poems. The letters are arranged to reflect the pattern of falling rain. A French actress named Marguerite Autant-Lara was once asked to read *Il pleut* to a group of friends. The actress was in despair when she failed to read the poem. It had to be transcribed into horizontal lines before it could be read aloud.

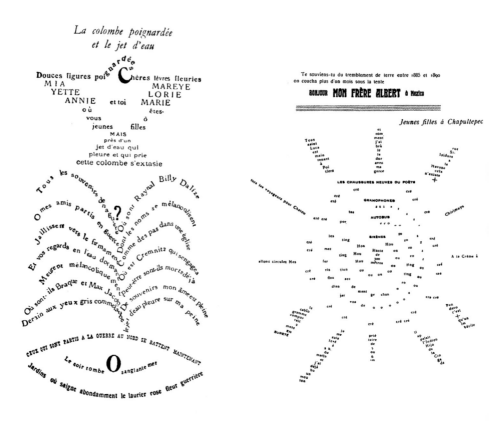

La colombe poignardée et le jet d'eau and *Lettres Océans* –
Guillaume Apollinaire
    Apollinaire's *Mon Frère Albert*, from the series of
    Lettres Océans is much more abstract in comparison
    to *La colombe poignardée et le jet d'eau*.

Que mon
Flacon
Me semble bon !
Sans lui
L'ennui
Me nuit,
Me suit.
Je sens
Mes sens
Mourants,
Pesants.
Quand je la tiens ,
Dieux ! que je suis bien !
Que son aspect est agréable !
Que je fais cas de ses divins présents !
C'est de son sein fécond, c'est de ses heureux flancs
Que coule ce nectar si doux, si délectable,
Qui rend tous les esprits, tous les cœurs satisfaits.
Cher objet de mes vœux, tu fais toute ma gloire.
Tant que mon cœur vivra, de tes charmants bienfaits
Il saura conserver la fidèle mémoire.
Ma muse à te louer se consacre à jamais,
Tantôt dans un caveau, tantôt sous une treille,
Ma lyre, de ma voix accompagnant le son,
Répétera cent fois cette aimable chanson :
'Règne sans fin, ma charmante bouteille ;
Règne sans cesse, mon flacon.

Rabelais Bottle – Charles-François Panard
This typographic arrangement by Charles-François Panard
(1694–1765) proves that visual poetry existed long before the
turn of the nineteenth century when figurative arrangements
of type became popular.

The Dada movement emerged from anarchist and socio-political initiatives in Zurich in 1915. The political neutrality of Switzerland throughout the First World War had lead to a sense of frustration amongst artists. Dadaism constituted a seemingly anti-functional approach to typography. As it was often devoid of any literal content, typography was reduced to a visual form of expression that, ironically, did not always result in the revelation of meaningful information. What seemed a medium without a message had in fact begun as a cynical response to what was perceived as a lack of common sense in politics. Dada quickly spread across Europe and reached as far as New York. **Kurt Schwitters** became one of the leading representatives in Germany. Similar to visual poetry, but in a less exclusive fashion, Dadaism helped to question many established conventions about graphical and typographical arrangements. By defying any notion of hierarchy in the composition of text and image elements, Dadaists aimed for a quasi-chaotic simultaneity of information fragments. This formal aesthetic anarchy was used as a means to encourage political criticism and to foster scepticism towards cultural settings. Later it inspired the surrealists.

'Invest your money in Dada! Dada is the only savings bank that pays interest in the hereafter!'
Kurt Schwitters

Kurt Schwitters

Kurt Schwitters was one of Germany's most prominent representatives of the Dada movement. Schwitters managed to combine artistic ambitions with commercial interests. He initiated the periodical *Merz*, which is an abbreviation of the German word *Kommerz*, and co-founded the Ring Neuer Werbegastalter, an association of advertising designers. Under the right-wing regime in Germany in the late 1930s Schwitters' work was considered as degenerate art. He emigrated to England in 1940 to flee the Nazi regime.

New Jersey Performing Arts Center – Paula Scher,
Pentagram Design

With her exterior design for the Lucent Technologies Center
for Arts Education in Newark, New Jersey, Scher took
typographic expression into the third dimension. Words,
which do not necessarily want to be read, cover the façade
making the building stand out from the surrounding brick-
wall architecture. The words wrap around the walls as if they
are staging their own energetic performance. Type becomes
pure attitude.

Despite the persistent popularity of Dada, there are very few contemporary designs truly comparable to works belonging to the movement. Paula Scher joined **Pentagram Design** as a partner in 1991. The promotional posters created for the Public Theater in New York in the late 1990s reflect some of the characteristics of Dadaist typography: type varies in size and weight and point in all possible directions. Letters and words, which are sometimes hand-drawn, move through the gaps, filling the page in an exuberant manner. As opposed to Dadaist collages, which were often black and white, colour is used to further enhance the visual agitation. Before being able to read a single word, the viewer is already overwhelmed by the explosive energy that lies behind the restless compositions.

Pentagram Design

Pentagram Design is a well-known international design consultancy with offices in London, Berlin, New York, Austin, and San Francisco. What makes Pentagram Design unique is its unusual business concept. About 20 partners work with their individual teams independent from one another in different parts of the world. The profits generated are shared equally between the partners at the end of the year. The name Pentagram derives from the fact that there were originally five partners who set up the company in London in 1972.

New York Public Theater – Paula Scher, Pentagram Design
Due to the intense competition in New York's theatre promotion and a growing similarity between poster styles, Scher redeveloped the visual identity of the Public Theater in 2008. Inspired by De Stijl graphics, she applied a much tamer approach by using text elements predominantly at a ninety-degree angle.

Futurist manifestos

Futurism was a rebellious movement that spread across many countries in Europe and influenced various forms of art including painting, architecture and music. Numerous manifestos appeared to spread radical messages in rejection of traditional principles, such as academic formalism and classical concepts of harmony. Futurists explicitly embraced energy and fearlessness – even war itself. Many of the futurists were very patriotic, so the interpretations of futurist principles often varied from one country to another.

'A new beauty has been added to the splendor of the world – the beauty of speed.'
Filippo Tommaso Marinetti

Futurists pushed the borderline of typography even further towards the virtually typographical. A distinction between text and image could often not be made anymore. By making reading often impossible, futurist collages forced the viewer to simply look at the accumulation of typographic fragments rather than to unveil their possible meaning through reading. To what degree a futurist piece of art was supposed to be considered an image, collage or typographic piece of art could often be determined only by the individual observer. Futurism originated in Italy where it was partly inspired by visual poetry. By turning typographic art into a less literal form of expression, futurists managed to escape the contextual constraints of poetic writing. Visual poetry became visual poetics. Futurism was an expressive response to industrialisation. It was meant to appeal to all members of society rather than just art lovers. Machines became the focal point of attention and the praise of speed the underlying agenda. Even though it originated in Italy, futurism had a widespread influence on art forms elsewhere in Europe. Whereas the **Futurist manifesto** was published in Milan in 1909, the *First Almanac of Futuristic Poetry* was issued in Warsaw in 1920. Filippo Tommaso Marinetti, the leader of the futurists in Milan, visited St Petersburg in 1910 and 1914 to present a series of lectures, spreading the influence eastwards.

Glory to the New Born King and *Imagine* – Alan Kitching

Alan Kitching is not a futurist designer. He is a contemporary
letterpress artist whose approach to design transcends
any style. However, the work shown here reflects some of
the characteristics of futurist typography. Type is placed at
dynamic angles; type sizes are varied to express a sense of
motion, growth and tension. Kitching printed *Glory to the
New Born King* (above left) with wood type on to translucent
Japanese paper. This poster belonged to a series that was
commissioned by a London music publisher for a Christmas
window display. *Dante's Inferno* (above right) is part of a
series of personal works for which Kitching printed coloured
type onto black paper. What appears as white here was
in fact type printed in silver. Kitching's use of colours and
overlapping letters goes well beyond what was seen in the
1920s, or in fact ever since.

Following the example of futurist principles, constructivism emerged in 1921 as a movement in post-revolutionary Russia. Even though artists in other parts of Europe thought along similar lines, it was here that art was pronounced 'dead' by Alexei Gan, one of the movement leaders. According to Gan, 'practical construction' was to replace 'the artist's speculative activity'. Instead of being art for the sake of art, constructivism was meant to serve the proletariat. It rejected individual stylistic ambitions in favour of the usefulness of the art or design object. As opposed to the western world, where public education had been made compulsory during the nineteenth century, there was still a high level of illiteracy in 1920s Russia. It was believed that graphic design based on geometric principles and a simplification of the Cyrillic script would be more accessible for Russia's public community. Paradoxically, this anti-stylistic functionalism was radical to such a degree that constructivism became undeniably an artistic style in its own right. Constructivism was not restricted to visual communication, it also formed a basis for painting, product design, architecture, film and so on. The range of Alexander Rodchenko's work reflects the diversity of constructivist disciplines on the one hand and the ambition to collectively support the new society on the other. As brief as it was, Rodchenko's contribution to constructivist typography was of great significance to modern typography.

'Art is dead! Let us cease our speculative activity (pictures) and take over the healthy basis of art – colour, line, materials, and forms – into the field of reality, of practical construction.'
<u>Alexei Gan</u>

Gosizdat – Alexander Rodchenko

Alexander Rodchenko created this advertising poster for the publishing house Gosizdat in 1924. It shows the actress Lilya Brik shouting out the word 'books'. Rodchenko was born in St Petersburg, Russia in 1891. He had moved from fine art to design in 1923, when he started to collaborate with the poet Vladimir Mayakovsky on advertising materials for diverse governmental trading organisations. He also worked for cultural institutions, focussing on graphic design for posters, books and films, until he returned to painting in the late 1930s.

De Stijl magazine – Theo van Doesburg

Together with Piet Mondrian, van Doesburg co-founded the movement De Stijl around a magazine publication with the same name. Two spreads of one issue of *De Stijl* magazine can be seen here next to its front and back cover. Today one might judge the composition as crude. Yet one can clearly see the inspiration from visual poetry that led to an exploration of type as a visual language. The cover pages reflect the rigorous domination of rectangular arrangements, typical of De Stijl. In the 1920s, van Doesburg distanced himself from Mondrian's point of view by acknowledging diagonals as acceptable elements.

Futurism was not the only inspiration for constructivism. The Dutch avant-garde movement De Stijl evolved around Theo van Doesburg's *De Stijl* magazine and was helped by Piet Mondrian's contribution. Much like visual poetry, De Stijl was, in a sense, self-motivated, inspired only by the work of contemporary painters. But whilst visual poetry rejected mechanisation, De Stjil embraced it. The geometric compositions used helped to develop rigorous guidelines for both product and visual design. Design had been stripped of any decorative elements. With its very controlled approach, De Stijl provided a kind of taming and anti-emotional influence on constructivism. Compared to the dynamic, expressive compositions of futurist art, De Stijl appeared rather calm and organised, dominated by the clarity of geometric forms. The formal aesthetics applied here showed a profound understanding of the dynamic relationship between compositional elements. Whilst futurism was an art form that reflected on industrialism, De Stijl became an industrialised form of art. As such, it had not only a crucial influence on Russian constructivism, but also on the agenda of the German Bauhaus school in the early 1920s.

'Our guiding principle was that design is neither an intellectual nor a material affair, but simply an integral part of the stuff of life, necessary for everyone in a civilized society.'
Walter Gropius

Van Doesburg first visited the Bauhaus in 1920. Only a few months later, he moved to Weimar hoping for a teaching position at the Bauhaus. Here, his influence helped to overcome the expressionist phase that dominated the beginning stage of the Bauhaus movement. With van Doesburg's growing influence, the interest of Bauhaus in constructivist approaches also rose, as did the ambition to turn art into production-art. With László Moholy-Nagy at his side, Walter Gropius, the first Bauhaus principal, established the Bauhaus school as a functionalist design institution. Herbert Bayer's *Universalschrift*, 1926, indicates the modernist ambition to find a pragmatic, universal concept of aesthetic expression. In 1928, both Gropius and Moholy-Nagy left the Bauhaus, on the basis that the Bauhaus was now sufficiently established.

Modernist functionalism

The second generation of modernists (those who practised visual design after the Second World War) understood functionalism in the conventional, pragmatic sense. The purpose behind typography was to deliver information quickly, i.e. efficiently. The aspect of aesthetic pleasure was considered to be secondary. The potential of visually challenging design solutions was limited, as they were often declared as artistic. The emphasis on visual clarity and communicative efficiency led to the rejection of emotive expression. This stands in contradiction to some of the early modernist movements, including Dadaism and Futurism. The question you should keep asking yourself when reading this book is in what way the emotive characteristics of typographic work affect the way typographic information is perceived by the information recipient.

Bauhaus – Anton Stankowski

Stankowski can be seen as a late modernist designer. He was born in 1906 in Germany, where he lived and worked until 1998. Despite the fact that he had no direct links with Bauhaus or De Stijl, Stankowski was much inspired by Mondrian's painting as well as by van Doesburg's work. Along with works of concrete art, Stankowski designed information materials and corporate identities, including the famously simple trademark for Deutsche Bank from 1974. The German publisher Taschen Verlag commissioned Stankowski to design the book jacket for Magdalena Droste's book on Bauhaus. No design solution could possibly reflect the Bauhaus ethos more appropriately than Stankowski's. The cover illustrates the Bauhaus preference for sans serif fonts and lower case writing. The rectangular pattern in primary colours shapes a lower case b.

bauhaus

bauhaus archiv   magdalena droste

1919
1933

TASCHEN

Following the Second World War, modern typography helped to promote the recovering industries. But modern typography itself did not develop much further. Many of the avant-garde movements mentioned suffered from the requirements of commercial industries. While the diverse interpretations of the modernist design principles sooner or later fell victim to the conservative constraints of the commercial world, poetry allowed various post-war typographers to escape commercial restrictions. Concrete poetry, which emerged in the 1950s, is often considered a late version of visual poetry. But most concrete poems are fundamentally different in their *modus operandi*. While visual poets challenged the words semantically, concrete poets visually interpreted their syntax. Concrete poets use the patterns of words, letters and punctuation marks to make statements. The word patterns are usually non-figurative. Using methodical structural processes to alter the arrangement of letters or words on a page, concrete poets relied on the experience of reading to convey a second level of meaning. As basic as the messages sometimes were, concrete poetry allowed readers to experience the process of reading *per se*, and exposed conventional reading as a highly stereotypical activity.

Selected works – Joshua Reichert

Reichert was born in Stuttgart, Germany, in 1937. He worked as a printer in his home town until studying at the Art Academy of Karlsruhe from 1956 to 1957. His studies incomplete, Reichert opened his own printing workshop in Stuttgart in 1960 but moved to Munich a year later. Along with his personal work, Reichert designs typographic information materials such as posters and announcements. He has become famous for his unusual visual poems, which he sometimes produces by pressing old wooden type on sheets of paper simply laid out on to the floor. The posters shown here illustrate how Reichert manages to challenge the functional aspects of typography to the extreme. Reichert's aesthetic arrangement of words complement their meaning.

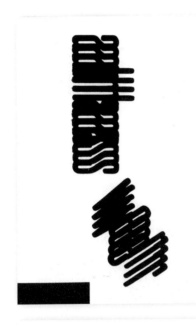

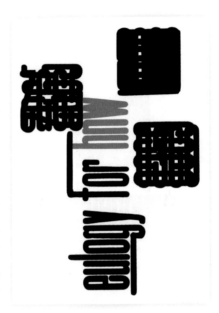

the black mystery
is   here
here   is
the black mystery

Selected works – Eugen Gomringer

Gomringer is a key figure in German concrete poetry. He was born in Bolivia in 1925 and studied economics and art history before he began to work at the University for Arts and Design in Ulm, Germany, in 1957. Gomringer founded his own press in 1960 to publish visual and concrete poetry. But whilst promoting the work of others, Gomringer also produced a significant body of poetic work himself. His approach to concrete poetry is very methodical: small modifications in the wording or in the arrangement of letters lead to puzzling results. It is easy to make sense of the words but difficult to determine their correct order. In 1976, Gomringer became Professor for Theory of Aesthetics at the Düsseldorf Arts Academy. This was followed by his appointment as Honorary Professor at the University of Applied Sciences in Zwickau, and in 2000 he established the Institute for Constructive Art and Concrete Poetry in Rihau together with his wife, Dr Nortrud Gomringer, and son, Stefan Gomringer.

Fisches
Nachtgesang

$$\text{—}$$
$$\cup \quad \cup$$
$$\text{—} \quad \text{—} \quad \text{—}$$
$$\cup \quad \cup \quad \cup \quad \cup$$
$$\text{—} \quad \text{—} \quad \text{—}$$
$$\cup \quad \cup \quad \cup \quad \cup$$
$$\text{—} \quad \text{—} \quad \text{—}$$
$$\cup \quad \cup \quad \cup \quad \cup$$
$$\text{—} \quad \text{—} \quad \text{—}$$
$$\cup \quad \cup \quad \cup \quad \cup$$
$$\text{—} \quad \text{—} \quad \text{—}$$
$$\cup \quad \cup$$
$$\text{—}$$

Fisches Nachtgesang – Christian Morgenstern

Morgenstern lived at the turn of the nineteenth century (1871–1914) in Germany. With most of his literary work intended as a comical comment on high literature, Morgenstern was, strictly speaking, not a concrete poet. In retrospect, however, his work is very interesting in relation to concrete poetry. For example, Morgenstern's *Fisches Nachtgesang* (1905) went beyond both the semantically and syntactically challenging approach of visual and concrete poetry. Can a poem that does not convey any linguistic components actually be considered a poem? Like the digital codes of software applications, *Fisches Nachtgesang* is pure syntax. There is no meaning beyond structure, yet in this particular case the structure itself still communicates a sense of irony. Where the level of abstraction is taken to such extremes that typographic signs can hardly be identified as such, we should speak of poetic expression rather than of poetry.

Computer networks connect people from different parts of the world. Today, this is done so efficiently that people are often left with little time to contemplate the information that is conveyed. Due to the information overload that results from the growing accessibility of information, visual perception is largely reduced to the registration of data. But information that is merely recognised as such does not communicate. People need time to reflect on information in order to generate an understanding, and they need to be given time to depict its visual presentation in order to appreciate its aesthetic appearance. Where information cascades, people can no longer appreciate the process of reading. The aesthetic pleasure is undermined by the time pressure. Virtual typography, as we shall see, may help to counteract this problem.

Cubico Stencil – Studio for Virtual Typography
This example of virtual typography shows a three-dimensional typeface named *Cubico Stencil*. The type appears more or less legible depending on the viewing angle. While the individual letters rotate, viewers are lured into guessing their signification. The aim behind virtual typography is to immerse the information recipient into the process of perception. This example also shows how light and spatial perspectives can be applied to achieve intriguing results with digital technologies.

Kinetic typography is not necessarily bound to digital media: it has gradually evolved from the design of film titles. This is why it is mostly associated with screen-based media. The expression 'kinetic typography' translates literally as 'the art of print in motion', which constitutes an interesting contradiction in terms. The printing of type is a fixation of texts, be it on to paper, on to a wall, or on to an object. So, exceptions aside, the text cannot really move. Obviously the carrying material or object may well be moving – it could be a car covered in advertising or simply the pages of a book. The reader may also be moving in relation to the text – when passing a billboard or a traffic sign, for example. However, the text would be interpreted as static rather than kinetic in each of those cases. Motion is generally perceived in relation to its context. Where a text moves in accordance to its surrounding, such as a car, the movement is attributed to the surrounding context – that is the car, not to the text itself. Kinetic typography, however, is type that is perceived to be in motion, so is synonymous with motion typography.

The term 'motion typography' is also mainly used for **screen-based communication**. Type can be set to move across the screen, the screen borders being the point of reference. A viewer would interpret the typography as motion typography in each of these cases. Unfortunately, a more liberal understanding of motion typography has entered the designer's vocabulary. It appears that any typographic information that changes over time is considered to be in motion, no matter whether its location changes or not. We need to differentiate between motion typography (type that moves) and transitional typography (gradually changing typography) in the following chapters.

Screen-based communication

This term encompasses computer screens and television screens, but also less obvious devices such as mobile telephones, personal digital assistants (PDAs) and car navigation systems. Screen-based communication is becoming increasingly dominant as digital displays begin to replace posters and printed signage systems.

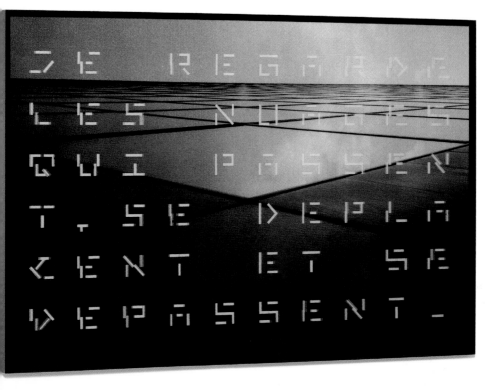

Open Sky – Studio for Virtual Typography

Horizons is a series of limited-edition prints. A layer of transitional type hovers above a photographic image of architectural structures. The type is more or less legible depending on the viewing angle. The plastic lens that is mounted on to the large-format print allows for the type to virtually fall apart as the viewer moves around the image. The text of each print in the series conveys philosophical reflections on contemporary urban life. The print shown here is entitled *Open Sky* and contemplates the movement of clouds in relation to the pace of modern life. This example of printed media defies the static nature of printed information. It shows that unconventional technical means can make it possible to introduce motion to print media.

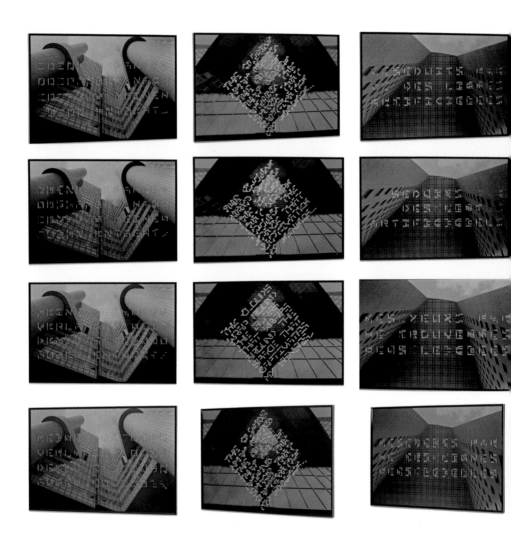

Desire, Mind Frame and *Vertigo* – Studio for Virtual Typography
The prints from the *Horizon* series shown on this page
use various languages to contemplate the way urban
surroundings can affect people's thoughts. They are
entitled *Desire* (above left) ('My thoughts long for that
which my eyes cannot reach...'); *Mind Frame* (above centre)
('The clouds wrap around the glass that wraps around the
space that captivates my senses...') and *Vertigo* (above
right) ('My eyes, which have been seduced by artificial
lines, search the sky in vain...'). The languages are chosen
in accordance to the country within which the buildings
featured in the background are found.

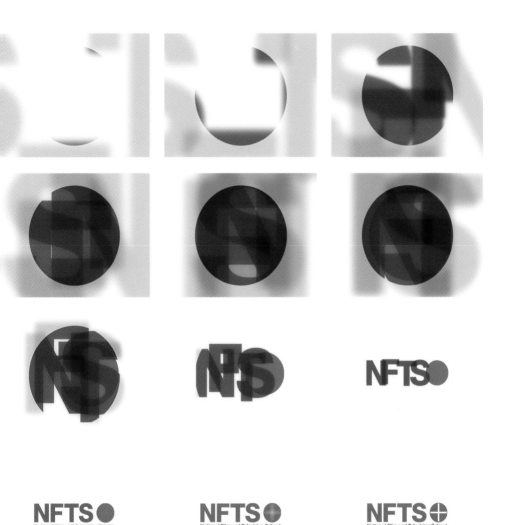

Time-based logotype – Studio for Virtual Typography
This logo animation was created for the National Film and Television School. The logotype was split into individual letters that move horizontally in an overlapping fashion. Due to their large size, the letters first appear as illegible graphic shapes. Eventually they become smaller and move into their accurate positions. During the process the motion graphic is masked so that only the circular area in the centre is coloured. Towards the end of the process, the circular shape transforms into the symbol that represents the institution. The typographic treatment here was inspired by Richard Greenberg's title sequence for the film *Altered States* (1980).

'Only that which is absent can be imagined.'
Marcel Proust

Temporal typography is a term that can be used synonymously with transitional typography to characterise typographic forms which change dynamically over time. Changes in type size, weight and position can be used in order to enhance the expressiveness of typographic messages. It is important to note that temporal or time-based typography does not accelerate the process of reading: it usually slows it down. But we may ask ourselves if it is at all beneficial to read at a fast pace. If we can argue that the pace of reading relates to the reader's memorisation of text, then we may assume that reading at a slow pace makes text information more memorable. One of the key advantages of transitional typography is that emotive expression can be enhanced by the definition of the graphic transition. A word written with a fairly standard-looking font can become expressive due to the way it changes over time.

Unfolded – Tomi Vollauschek

Tomi Vollauschek, who co-founded the London-based design agency FL@33 in London in 2001, created this animated typeface in 1999 when he studied at the Royal College of Art in London. The type evolves from diamond-shaped graphic elements which virtually unfold into squares, then into lines, and finally into letter shapes. The end result is a simple pixel font. But the transition, which is accompanied by a subtle flapping sound, lends the typeface an entertaining, humorous quality. Vollauschek's AAT (acoustic animated typeface) application, which includes an animated display of Unfolded, can be downloaded for free from the FL@33 website <www.flat33.com>.

'Although we are currently undergoing a sea change in the dissemination of information, from paper to all of these new things that are not paper, the messages themselves remain stubbornly typographic. As long as we still speak and think with language, we will continue to read and write and therefore, typography will play a role.'
David Small

Information landscapes are computer-generated environments that allow users to navigate virtually through the information that is displayed on screen. Texts and images are essentially static here. It is the reader who moves virtually through three-dimensiona arrangements of blocks of text similar to the interactive navigation used in many computer games. In his essay *Navigating Large Bodies of Text*, David Small documents a concept that originated at the **Massachusetts Institute of Technology** (MIT) in the mid-1990s. Small's article discusses various cognitive problems in relation to the perception of three-dimensional texts within a digital environment. Confusion arises, for example, where users are confronted with the reverse side of a block of text. Overlapping text appearing from various angles can add to this visual irritation. Small also explains that greeking, a technique that allows for small or virtually distant lines of text to be replaced with grey lines, can help to improve the presentation of multi-dimensional typographic compositions.

Massachusetts Institute of Technology (MIT)

The MIT is a US-based private university that emphasises scientific and technological research. Its Aesthetics + Computation Group is renowned for producing outstanding computer application for communication purposes. The Visible Language Workshop, founded by Muriel Cooper and Ron MacNeil in 1973, was another considerably influential initiative of the MIT.

Typotown – HeiWid

Typotown is a playful, interactive, three-dimensional environment made exclusively from type. Users can view the towering letters from diverse angles. Moving the cursor allows users to move forwards, backwards, and left and right. The user interface allows changes to the typeface, type colour and the transparency of letters. Users can also define the four-letter word that shapes the virtual buildings. The application does not lend itself to communicating text messages, but through changing the display settings, the user can produce an infinite amount of graphics. HeiWid (short for Heinz Widmer) created this online application with Lingo script in Macromedia Director, a multimedia application that has been largely superseded by Adobe Flash. HeiWid works in Bern, Switzerland, where he co-runs a design consultancy called Büro Destruct together with his partners. _Typotown_ can be found on the company's website <www.burodestruct.net>.

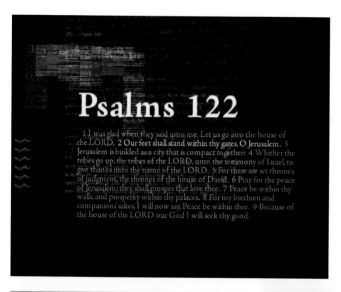

Talmud Project – David Small

David Small's *Talmud Project* was produced at the MIT media laboratory. It combines text passages from the *Torah*, the first five books of the Hebrew Bible, and the *Talmud*, a sacred book of the Jewish faith. The blocks of text can be arranged interactively to shape walls through which the reader can navigate. Different text connections can be made according to the reader's preference. The success of this design solution relies on people's real-life familiarity with architectural environments.

Financial Viewpoint – Lisa Strausfeld, Pentagram Design
Lisa Strausfeld is an expert in media installations. She worked as a research assistant in the Visible Language Workshop before co-founding the information architecture software company, Perspecta, along with two of her MIT classmates. Strausfeld joined Pentagram Design New York as a partner in 2002 and has thus extended the company's portfolio with her interaction design work. This project shows how the concept of information landscapes can be implemented into a commercial context. Three-dimensionality is used to organise complex data relating to a variety of funds. This allows the user to access the selected information from multiple perspectives, each of which reveal two-dimensional information such as graphs and charts.

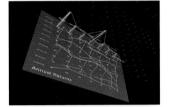

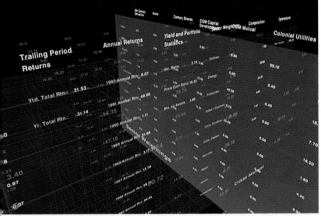

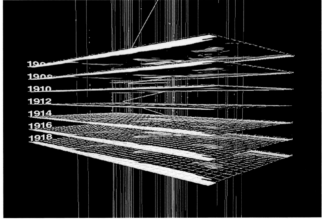

The Millennium Project – Lisa Strausfeld, Pentagram Design

The Millennium Project is a three-dimensional timeline that uses one direction as a timescale and the remaining two for geographical data. The location of the information within its three-dimensional system environment tells users what happened where in the world and at what time in history. It also reveals other events that occurred at around the same time, so the user can virtually travel through time and space and access text and image-based information in accordance with the three-dimensional coordinates of the journey.

Designers usually try to achieve user satisfaction through clarity and ease of information access. But it is the challenge attached to navigating information landscapes that makes them exciting. Any new kind of text presentation asks for a new mode of perception. At first glance, an information landscape looks strange and obscure. The reader must re-orientate to extract the information; a fascinating process. If we are correct in assuming that virtual typography has a fundamentally new aesthetic quality, then we may expect to find it in the certain strangeness of its visual presentation, and this strangeness evolves from its time-based disposition.

The gradual uncovering of meanings requires a different mode of text presentation from that which is fostered by conventional hypertext. The timing of information determines its aesthetic quality because it prepares the information recipient for the content. The mode of transition can therefore be seen as an aesthetic element that is attached to the verbal information content.

With their interactive installation, *Streams of Consciousness*, David Small and Tom White 'hoped to evoke the fluid contents of conscious memory'. Philosophically, it may appear strange that the artists offered the user the interactive control of their flow of consciousness. Isn't it precisely the unpredictability that makes the natural flow of water so intriguing? Isn't it the fact that we do not fully understand the growth of a tree that makes it appear beautiful? We can only sense an underlying logic to its shape and form. It is this moment of speculation that triggers fascination and sustains attention, be it in relation to nature, or to verbal and visual means of communication.

Streams of Consciousness – David Small and Tom White
This computational exercise uses moving text elements
to simulate the flow of water. A manual user interface allows
users to stop the flow of words, to push or pull individual
words and to change the words altogether. The title of
this work hints at the dilemma surrounding multimedia
typography. The computational arguments focus on
technological production and conscious communication.
The unconscious or preconscious perception of information
remains neglected. In order to understand the aesthetics
of virtual typography, we need to examine the way in which
information is expected to evolve from ambiguity into
meaning over time.

To improve the screen-based communication of typographic information we should think of **virtual** typography as information that is nearly or virtually typographical, rather than defining virtual typography simply as computer-generated type, or as type that is displayed through computer technologies. What appears virtually typographical constitutes ambiguous information. This means that virtual typography does not operate on the borderline of legibility like postmodern typography. Instead, virtual typography challenges the viewer during the recognition stage that precedes the reading process. The word 'viewer', by the way, is chosen with care here. The viewer becomes a reader precisely when typographic forms become legible. This transitional stage, however, follows the point in time where information is identified as typographic. This moment of identification is the very instant when we consider text to be virtually typographical. Depending on the circumstances and the perceptual capabilities of the individual observer, this moment can occur sooner or later during the process of transition. It can even occur where non-typographical information is wrongly perceived as typographical.

The virtual

From a philosophical point of view, we must acknowledge that 'the virtual' stands in juxtaposition to 'the actual', not to 'the real'. In other words, 'the virtual' exists for real, even though it is not, or not yet, physically present. This means that the term 'virtual' can be attributed to anything that is expected to appear or evolve. 'The virtual' is what is possibly real, even though it is 'not actually there'.

'That which is virtual does not as such contradict that which is real. It opposes that which is "actually" there.'
Pierre Lévy

Modernism versus postmodernism

Typography is mostly aimed at making reading easier. Modernist designers placed legibility high on their agenda. Postmodernists rebelled against this functionalist principle. It is striking that postmodern typography became popular when digital technologies were introduced to graphic design in the 1980s (we will discuss this period in more depth later). It is important to note that legibility was disputed in a particularly intensive fashion during the 1980s, when computational developments promoted the acceleration of information transmission. Postmodernists, who argued against the modernist emphasis on legibility, often failed to develop a sufficient rationale for their visual solutions. They often took refuge in the notion of intuitive and therefore inexplicable design practice. By examining the borderline between text and image, this book will help to shed new light on the postmodern principle of visual ambiguity.

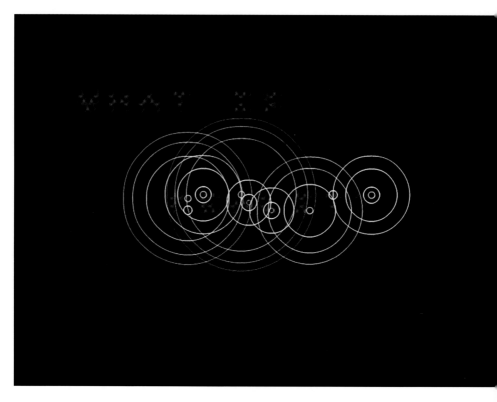

Automotive Hydraulic – Studio for Virtual Typography
These stills show a music video developed for Loca
Records in Brighton, UK. Inspired by movement in nature,
the text appears through transitions that remind the viewer
of raindrops and air bubbles moving through water. Much
of the footage used was created digitally. As most of the
content is of a typographic nature, the video passages are
also often perceived as virtual typography, even though the
coloured lines were created through long exposure shots of
artificial lights in the street at night. This misinterpretation
of information shows the extent to which visual perception
relies on the viewer's expectations. The text is the English
translation of a German concrete poem written by Helmut
Heissenbüttel (a Chinese reader stated that the graphic in
the fifth still resembles a Chinese character when written in
cursive writing, an ancient style of Chinese). Depending on
the context, one would read either 'thing' or 'event'.
It appears as if the borderline between image and text
remains in question.

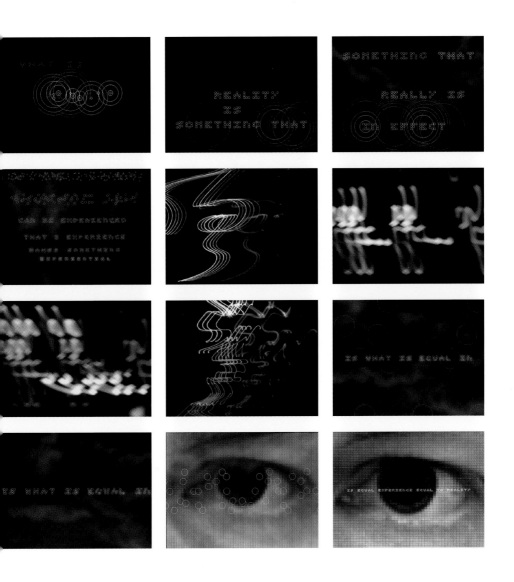

Creative industries often tend to treat the terms 'information design' and 'communication design' as synonymous. However, the difference is crucial if we want to understand how virtual typography stimulates the viewer's senses. The confusion between information design and communication design probably derives from the widespread emphasis on the creation of information designs. Information is produced for the purpose of communication. From a perceptual point of view the situation is less straightforward because not all information communicates. Information in the context of communication theory is nothing but 'noise' that is subject to the interpretation of the information recipient. The viewer's reconstruction of meaningful content is a complex process.

Chain Reaction – David Lozano
David Lozano, who graduated from the London College of Communication (LCC) in 2006, is now working as a freelance designer in London. For *Chain Reaction*, Lozano used a vast amount of matches to construct the word 'flamboyant'. This final-year project constitutes a very courageous attempt to examine the dynamic relationship between the form and the content of a word through a process of destruction. When the piece was set on fire, a new image evolved, quite literally overpowering the meaning of the word. What is left as a result is a two-metre-long piece of type, the remains of which tell the story of its making.

Before analysing the perception of typography we need to consider that typographic communication extends beyond perceptual issues to emotive responses, intellectual reflection and, of course, the reader's ability to memorise information. As part of the perception process that precedes these reactive activities, we can differentiate between three stages: a) the cognition of data (registration of signals); b) the recognition of information (classification of information) and c) the process of decoding (for example, reading). These three stages usually happen in close succession and will often be felt as instant. Situations where we misperceive information make us aware of the complexity of the perception process that relates to reading. The ambiguity that is often inherent in strong design solutions tends to provoke a moment of rest because it invites viewers to examine the work more closely.

Cognition of data

In order to communicate, information must first be identified as such. This means that it must be filtered from random, irrelevant signals. During this initial cognition stage, signals that appear to be potentially significant are selected for closer consideration, establishing a focus of attention. This cognitive stage is particularly interesting in the context of **transitional information** such as virtual typography. Where the time-span for perceiving information is very limited (due to the transitional nature of the information, for example), the viewer needs to set, and possibly reset, his or her focus of attention quickly.

Classification

Following the cognition of information, a process of classification takes place. Here the viewer separates typographic from graphic or photographic information. Images are scanned differently to texts. When confronted with a foreign writing system, we realise that this process

Transitional information

The scenario of watching transitional information can be compared to driving through a city at night. Here the driver is confronted with a plenitude of signals such as road signs, traffic lights and other vehicles. The speed at which the relevant information needs to be filtered from the vast amount of signals available forces the driver to ignore certain kinds of data such as advertorial neon lights or illuminated windows – these are registered but not consciously perceived. A passenger experiences the same scenario very differently. As he or she is not responsible for the safety of the journey, the passenger would usually apply a much more lateral mode of perception. This shows on the one hand that a lot of information fails to communicate because it remains ignored. On the other, the example also reveals what information communicates and what does not: it depends much on the intentions and interests of the information recipient. If designers wish to do justice to the expectation of their target audience, they need to take the viewer's intentions into account because these direct their focus of attention.

of classification is much more difficult than when we are looking at a written language with which we are familiar. Chinese script, for example, is scanned in a different way to the Roman alphabet. Images are generally scanned in a much more random way than plain texts. So before being able to read we need to determine the appropriate code by testing different possible scanning patterns. Virtual typography turns this process of classification into a perceptual challenge in which readers can be forced to repeatedly readjust their scanning pattern. They can never be certain what kind of information, text or image, will follow later on during the time-based information display.

Decoding

Once aware of the presence of information, as well as of its classification, the information recipient can begin decoding or – in the case of text – deciphering the information. Considering that multimedia is a hybrid of various conventional media such as cinematography, animation, graphic design and typography, we need to acknowledge that typography is more or less a hybrid of text and image. From a design perspective a typographic message is composed rather than written. The arrangement of words, sentences and blocks lends the text an image-like quality. Due to its metalinguistic architectural characteristics, typography is scanned as well as read. Barely legible typography forces the reader to scan a piece of text repeatedly.

'Information pours upon us, instantaneously and constantly.'
Marshall McLuhan

Marshall McLuhan (1911–1980), a communications theorist and a philosopher from Canada, coined various well-known expressions such as 'the medium is the message' and 'global village'. Most of his theories were aimed at pre-electronic media such as radio and television. His arguments, which were at times considered to be controversial, could easily be applied to computer technologies and McLuhan's writing has influenced many contemporary media philosophers.

<u>Posters</u> – Reza Abedini

These posters designed by Reza Abedini (from Iran), show typographic information written in Farsi. A viewer unfamiliar with Middle-Eastern languages is bound to get stuck during the recognition stage of the perception process. Classifying the information as typographic is impossible without knowing the typographic origin of the signs used. But even readers of Iranian origin tend to be puzzled by Abedini's typographic creations. One needs to spend extra time searching for the text within the arrangement of linguistic symbols. Thus the reading phase is deliberately delayed to allow for a moment of aesthetic contemplation.

The first poster (above left) illustrates the intertwined names of Mehran Mohajer (a photographer) and Abedini himself. This poster was designed to advertise a joint exhibition of both lecturers.

The second poster (above right) announces a lecture that Abedini held in front of an audience of 400 designers at his home in 2003. The dark type in the background reflects his large audience. The highlighted type shown slightly off-centre represents Abedini speaking on stage.

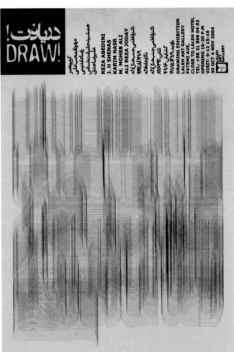

The third poster (above left) was created to advertise a group drawing exhibition. The words, which are systematically repeated here, form a pattern that reveals the forenames of the four exhibitors: Reza, Mehrdad, Karim and Jamshid.

The final poster (above right) features the word 'Sima', a term that can be translated as 'portrait', 'visual' or 'image'. This poster advertised an exhibition that used four digital projections of designs and photographic images. The visitor was surrounded by the works on display.

Abedini taught and practised typography in Tehran until he moved to Amsterdam, Holland, in 2008. But he also has an academic background in painting. His experience as a painter may explain to some extent the extraordinary quality of his typographic compositions. Abedini does not consider himself an artist, but his art education has allowed him to develop an unconventional perspective on typographic compositions. His unique typographic works appear like typographic sculptures within two dimensions.

Even though static typography can challenge readers to scan a piece of text more than once, the image–text relationship is clear as soon as the information has been classified correctly. What cannot technically transform cannot **epistemologically** be expected to change in shape. Ornamental, modern or postmodern typography may make reading a difficult task. It may even delay the classification of information. But it cannot repeatedly challenge the viewer's expectations towards evolving signals. Text remains a text, an image remains an image and a piece of figurative type remains a piece of figurative type. Time-based media operates differently. Transitional typography allows for words and letters to emerge from and to dissolve into random signals, so viewers are continually challenged to predict the kind of information that is about to evolve.

Epistemology

This term stems from the Greek words *episteme*, which means 'knowledge', and *logos*, which means 'word' or 'speech'. This branch of philosophy deals with the origins of knowledge. Through studying the sources of our rational understanding of the world, epistemologists aspire to resolve how we assess what is true and what is not, and how we justify our knowledge of the world.

Time-based information – Kate Moross

Before entering her undergraduate training, Moross created an example of motion graphics that was quite unusual due to its consistent ambiguity between moving image and moving type. The project was presented during the 'Typo.move' conference, which was organised by onedotzero at the Institute of Contemporary Arts (ICA) in London in 2005. Even the trained eye keeps struggling to detect the typographic signs within the constellation of various rotating circle sections. The classification of information is turned into a guessing game here and reading becomes an aesthetic challenge. One is inclined to think that some of the circles might not convey any letters, so the tension is sustained. Moross's example is particularly intriguing because the typographic nature of the information cannot be determined on the basis of individual stills due to the level of visual abstraction. Only the succession of several frames allows the viewer to correctly categorise the information as typographic.

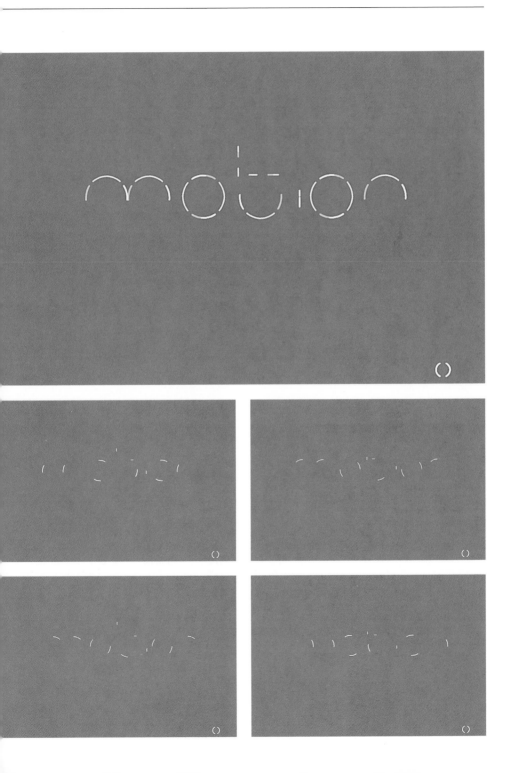

Intelligibility is the degree to which words or sentences appear familiar and are comprehensible. Considering the fact that information does not necessarily consist of legible or intelligible signs, we may claim that Dadaist typography (as discussed on pages 18–21) was perfectly informational. Dadaist collages provided text information, often without explicitly communicating any message, yet the information was both recognisable (classifiable) as well as readable (decodable). However, it was often devoid of any syntax (orderly structure) so that the words and letters did not always convey any meaningful message. In other words, it was not always intelligible. This means that we need to add a fourth communicative stage to the three mentioned above: the understanding of information (intelligibility) follows the cognition (registration or selection of data), the recognition (classification) and the decoding of information (reading). The fact that Dadaist work was able to communicate an attitude despite the lack of syntax reveals that the quality of typographic communication should not be measured exclusively by the successful delivery of a verbal message. The aesthetic characteristics of typographic work direct the viewer's attention, and prepare them emotionally for the message that is to be read. Thus the aesthetic quality can be just as important as its literal message content.

Kleine Dada Soirée – Theo van Doesburg

Theo van Doesburg co-founded the De Stijl group (see pages 26–27) but also explored other art movements, such as Dadaism. This example illustrates how excessive amounts of information can lead to visual confusion. Much of the information escapes the viewer's rational understanding. Words that are seen are not necessarily read. Words that are read are not necessarily understood. However, Dadaist work was not always meant to communicate text information explicitly, rather to express a general attitude towards society and politics.

When observing time-based media, viewers cannot be certain about which kind of information they are going to be presented with. Yet if graphic elements are used to hint at potential information, expectations arise towards the process of transformation. Viewers are thus motivated to make predictions about evolving forms of expression. This future-oriented perception is not possible with static information, because no changes may be expected.

The relationship between consecutive images
The sense of a continuously changing relationship between visual elements (the progressive nature of transitional information) affects the viewer's expectations over time. This is why motion graphics have a fundamentally different aesthetic quality to still images. The relationship between consecutive images plays a vital role in the perception of transitional typography because it continuously changes the viewer's mindset. To put it bluntly, we may say that the whole is greater than the sum of its parts. But what exactly is 'the whole'? **Gilles Deleuze** explains that 'If one had to define the whole, it would be defined by "Relation"' (Deleuze, 2001). According to Deleuze, 'Relation' constitutes an entity that exists between 'objects'. Where this relation between objects changes, 'the whole' is transformed. 'The whole' remains unchanged when people look at static typography because the relationship between the typographic elements remains static. With virtual typography, 'the whole' changes constantly. The need for the continuous reinterpretation of the changing information requires the viewer to

Gilles Deleuze

Gilles Deleuze (1925–1995), a Parisian philosopher, defined 'the virtual' as an idea that exists in relation to a difference that transcends time and space. Following his famous publication *Anti-Oedipus*, which he co-authored with Félix Guattari, Deleuze wrote two books in the 1980s about the nature of film: *Cinéma I: L'image-mouvement* and *Cinéma II: L'image-temps*.

constantly adjust the mode of perception. This is an important aspect in the aesthetic perception of virtual typography because it remotivates the level of attention paid in the course of the information display. The constant fluctuation between image and text keeps the viewer in suspense and lends virtual typography its immersive quality.

Saussure's semiological concept of the signifier and the signified (see page 14) has determined the designers' understanding of typographic communication for many decades. But the model that once helped us understand the difference between text and image now limits us in understanding the relationship between the two in the context of virtual type. If we want to analytically approach the difference between virtual typography and static typography, we need to acknowledge the fact that virtual typography is not necessarily digital even though it lends itself to being used in digital environments. Two things make virtual typography special, different and separate from conventional print or screen typography: a) the deliberate delay in its communicative function and b) its temporary disguise as abstract imagery.

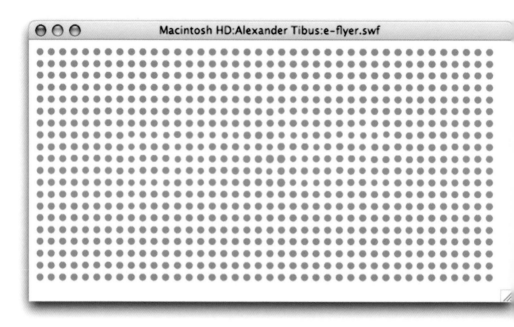

Dancing Type – Alexander Tibus

Alexander Tibus, a freelance designer based in Berlin, Germany, uses a fluctuating level of contrast between text and background to display the words 'prêt à danser' to advertise a music venue. Tibus creates this contrast by gradually changing the size of the dots within a rectangular dot pattern. The dots that shape the letters become larger at first, then smaller than the surrounding ones, which change conversely in size. The figure–ground relationship is continuously dynamic and therefore seduces the viewer into an informational guessing game. It seems as if the mind is always reaching slightly further than the eye can see. As opposed to Moross's work, stills can be extracted here to show the text more or less clearly. However, when perceived in motion, the typographic transition provokes an aesthetic response that is fundamentally different from that which we apply to a series of screen grabs. See Tibus's flyer online <www.alexandertibus.de/Resources/eflyer.swf>.

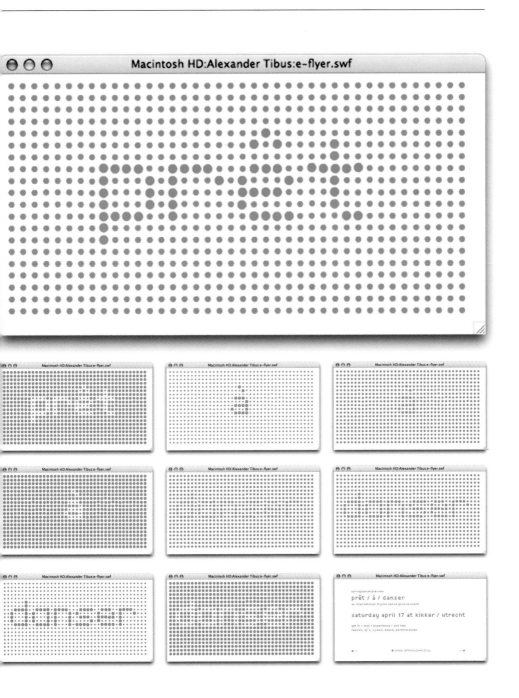

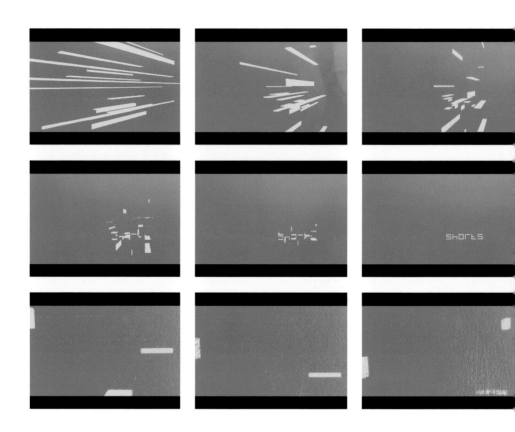

Delayed communication

The different stages of the communication discussed earlier help us to understand that time is needed for any communicative activity. Yet, virtual typography can delay transitions in excess of the time required for decoding information. Thus, virtual typography acts in a disturbing fashion. If we want to attribute syntax to virtual typography, we must assume an evolving, (time-based, structural) rule that is initially unknown to the viewer. The novelty value of this time-based code provokes discomfort and tension. This tension, however, is of an aesthetic nature, and it stands in opposition to stress caused by information overload. The stretching of the transitional process, which the viewer requires for determining the syntax, causes a decompression of time. While the eye traces the continuity of motion, the mind aspires to detect its function. As opposed to hypertext, which fragments not only the content of text, but also its temporal structure, virtual typography reinforces the sense of a temporal continuity.

'Of what value are typographic choices – bold and italics, for example – when words can dance across the screen, dissolve or disappear altogether?'
Jessica Helfand

Shorts – Rudd Studio

Rudd Studio is a young London-based design agency specialising in brand identities. With a team of three, Matt Rudd has created a lot of work for the television sector. His introductory sequence to a Film4 television series entitled *Shorts* plays with the conflicting relationship between continuity and fragmentation. The word 'Shorts' evolves gradually from a pattern of elongated lines that turn by 90 degrees. The first draft version of this animation showed a continuous transition of the line pattern. In his assumption that consistency in transition would not offer enough visual stimulation, Rudd inserted a close-up section to disrupt the continuity of change and to increase the visually confusing effect. Thus Rudd replaced the very moment where the word becomes recognisable as a typographic piece of information. The passage where the image pattern turns into virtual type has thus been hidden and the graphic part becomes separated from the typographic phase. The temporal continuity has here been replaced with the succession of two events.

Channel 4 – Brett Foraker

UK television channel Channel 4's on-air brand identity, which was launched in 2005, was created and produced in-house. Following his appointment as Network Creative Director at Channel 4, Brett Foraker decided to apply a highly innovative approach to reintroduce the original Channel 4 logo from 1982. Using some of the latest special effect techniques the logo was digitally constructed in the shape of various three-dimensional objects, which were virtually integrated into film footage. These typographic transformations are very rigorous in terms of the continuity of motion. Not only does the pace of transition remain perfectly consistent throughout, but by shaping the number '4' with real-life objects (pylons, neon signs, hedges, for example), the viewer's chances of missing the point at which the image becomes typographic are also further increased. Therefore most viewers will be keen to review the sequence at least once or twice in order to be able to detect the logo.

The temporary image aspect

As explained previously, an image-like quality is attached to more or less any typographic composition. The difference between static and transitional typography is that in the latter case the image aspect is dynamic. If we look at typography as an amalgam of text and image, then the dominance between the two fundamentally different forms of communication may shift from one to the other. Rather than simply altering the spatial arrangement (for example, the typographic composition over time), virtual typography involves a change in the nature of information. As text elements move across the screen, it is not the image aspect of a typographic arrangement that changes, rather that the text elements evolve directly from the image. In other words, virtual typography results from changing the formal representation of meaning itself, rather than from simply changing the location of its different components, such as images, words, or individual letters.

'Ours is a brand-new world of allatonceness. "Time" has ceased, "space" has vanished. We now live in a global village ... a simultaneous happening.'
Marshall McLuhan

The phenomenon of gradually evolving type existed long before the introduction of digital mass media in the 1980s. The question is, therefore, not to what degree digital technologies may facilitate or improve the creation of virtual typography, but how virtual typography can help to compensate for the problems that evolve from the use of digital communication technologies. How can it help to reinstate the time space that is so significant for communication, and how can it help to decompress the information density that makes digital media so stressful to use?

Channel 4 – Brett Foraker
Together with his team (Gwilym Gwillim (Producer), Adam Rudd (Editor), Sean Costelloe (Post-production Producer), Russell Appleford (3D Special Effects Supervisor) and Rich Martin (Sound Designer)), Foraker created a considerable number of variations using a different theme each time. The Channel 4 brand campaign was awarded the D&AD Black Pencil, one of the world's most prominent design awards.

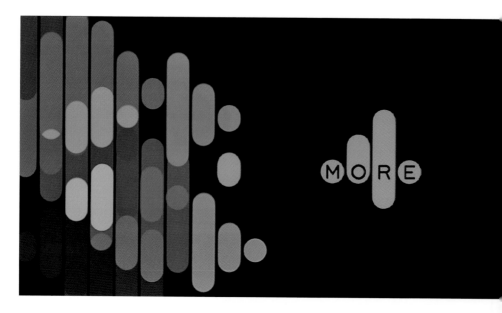

More4 – Brett Foraker, Jason Smith and Spin
Digital television channel More4's campaign uses a
photographic image scenario for embedding the typographic
elements. However, drawing a line between image and type
becomes even more difficult where the image component is
abstract to begin with. The More4 campaign is the result of
a close collaboration between Brett Foraker, Jason Smith of
Fontsmith in London, and Spin, the agency that created the
visual identity for More4. The television identity uses nothing
but graphic shapes to construct a logo over time. It is striking
how the minimalist composition of the More4 logo lends itself
to extensive variations in its graphic animation. The level of
ambiguity is again taken to extremes. The number
4 is difficult to recognise even when its graphic components
come to a halt. In the process of its transition, the word
'more' appears bit by bit within the shape of the number
4 through a process of degressive masking.

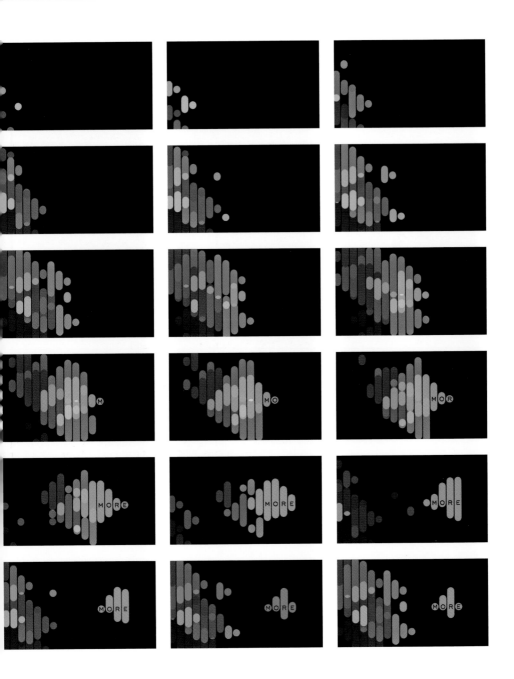

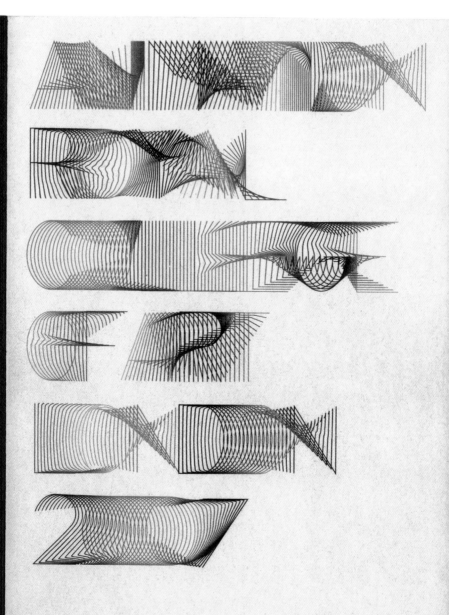

Digital technologies triggered a fundamental change during the 1980s. Digital typography and desktop publishing have since led to the fusion of various production-related tasks in the field of visual design. Since the introduction of desktop computers, individual users have increasingly tried to master multiple specialist tasks such as type design, layout, illustration and production management. As a result, the significance of the graphic designer changed dramatically: the designer could feasibly now technically cover a larger variety of tasks, but his professional status became increasingly threatened by amateurs who could operate the necessary software applications. In fact, the distinction between professional designers and amateurs could often hardly be made.

Type in transition – Royal College of Art
This typographic solution was created in 2007 for the catalogue and the showreel of the Animation Department at the Royal College of Art (RCA) in London. Filip Tydén (from Sweden) and Hugo Timm (from Brazil) were still students at the RCA when they made a successful bid for the job. This remarkable design shows how computer-generated typographic transitions can be transferred effectively on to print media. Each of the letters on the cover blends into the following. Even though reading becomes a challenge, a certain degree of legibility is sustained. It is always important to bear in mind the target audience for evaluating the appropriateness of barely legible solutions. This design mainly addresses people who are interested in art, design and animation. To turn the typographic information into a perceptual challenge is therefore not only adequate; it is also visually compelling. Following their graduation in 2008, Tydén and Timm have teamed up with Valerio Di Lucente from Italy and Erwan Lhuissier from France to set up their own design studio called Julia in London.

The digital era in design began in 1983, when Apple introduced the Apple Lisa, the first desktop computer with a graphical user interface (GUI). This enabled users to operate computers intuitively with the help of pop-up windows and drop-down menus. Apple Lisa was followed by the release of the first Apple Macintosh in 1984. Its sales improved vastly in the following year when the Apple LaserWriter, the first laser printer (sold in the US in 1985 at $6,995), and Aldus PageMaker, the first layout software application, entered the market. Aesthetically, however, the digitally created artwork suffered an initial setback. The memory capacities of the first Apple computers were very limited (128 kilobytes), and the size of the monochrome display was restricted to nine inches (512 x 342 pixels). Even though Apple licensed Adobe's PostScript (a code that enables vector-based outlines to rasterise effectively) as early as 1985, it was not until 1989 that PostScript was distributed internationally and recognised as an industry standard. Therefore many designers had to rely on **dot matrix printers**, which did not offer any satisfying output.

Dot matrix printer

Dot matrix printers use pins that strike against an ink-soaked cloth ribbon in order to transfer a fine pattern of dots on to paper. The output quality process, which is similar to that of typewriters, is very poor by comparison to laser or contemporary inkjet printers. For this reason, dot matrix printers are now rarely used.

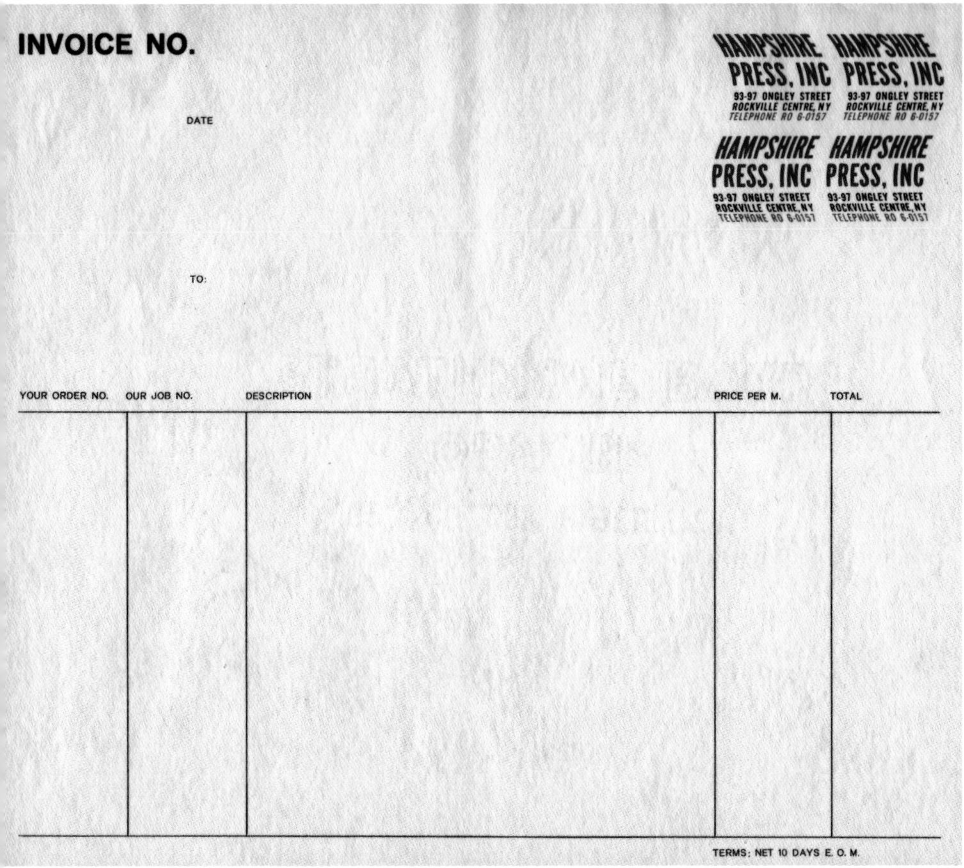

INVOICE NO.

DATE

TO:

HAMPSHIRE PRESS, INC
93-97 ONGLEY STREET
ROCKVILLE CENTRE, N Y
TELEPHONE RO 6-0157

HAMPSHIRE PRESS, INC
93-97 ONGLEY STREET
ROCKVILLE CENTRE, N Y
TELEPHONE RO 6-0157

HAMPSHIRE PRESS, INC
93-97 ONGLEY STREET
ROCKVILLE CENTRE, N Y
TELEPHONE RO 6-0157

HAMPSHIRE PRESS, INC
93-97 ONGLEY STREET
ROCKVILLE CENTRE, N Y
TELEPHONE RO 6-0157

YOUR ORDER NO.	OUR JOB NO.	DESCRIPTION	PRICE PER M.	TOTAL

TERMS: NET 10 DAYS E. O. M.

Hampshire Press – Chermayeff & Geismar
This New York design agency was born when Tom Geismar joined the already existing partnership between Robert Brownjohn and Ivan Chermayeff in 1957. Brownjohn left the company two years later to work independently in London. This visual identity for the Hampshire Press shows how the design group explored means of distortion long before computers came to dominate production processes.

Metro Typographers Incorporated 27 West 24th Street New York 10 Telephone Watkins 9-6290
Metro Typographers Incorporated 27 West 24th Street New York 10 Telephone Watkins 9-6290
Metro Typographers Incorporated 27 West 24th Street New York 10 Telephone Watkins 9-6290
Metro Typographers Incorporated 27 West 24th Street New York 10 Telephone Watkins 9-6290
Metro Typographers Incorporated 27 West 24th Street New York 10 Telephone Watkins 9-6290
Metro Typographers Incorporated 27 West 24th Street New York 10 Telephone Watkins 9-6290
Metro Typographers Incorporated 27 West 24th Street New York 10 Telephone Watkins 9-6290
Metro Typographers Incorporated 27 West 24th Street New York 10 Telephone Watkins 9-6290
Metro Typographers Incorporated 27 West 24th Street New York 10 Telephone Watkins 9-6290
Metro Typographers Incorporated 27 West 24th Street New York 10 Telephone Watkins 9-6290
Metro Typographers Incorporated 27 West 24th Street New York 10 Telephone Watkins 9-6290
Metro Typographers Incorporated 27 West 24th Street New York 10 Telephone Watkins 9-6290
Metro Typographers Incorporated 27 West 24th Street New York 10 Telephone Watkins 9-6290
Metro Typographers Incorporated 27 West 24th Street New York 10 Telephone Watkins 9-6290
Metro Typographers Incorporated 27 West 24th Street New York 10 Telephone Watkins 9-6290
Metro Typographers Incorporated 27 West 24th Street New York 10 Telephone Watkins 9-6290
Metro Typographers Incorporated 27 West 24th Street New York 10 Telephone Watkins 9-6290
Metro Typographers Incorporated 27 West 24th Street New York 10 Telephone Watkins 9-6290
Metro Typographers Incorporated 27 West 24th Street New York 10 Telephone Watkins 9-6290
Metro Typographers Incorporated 27 West 24th Street New York 10 Telephone Watkins 9-6290
Metro Typographers Incorporated 27 West 24th Street New York 10 Telephone Watkins 9-6290
Metro Typographers Incorporated 27 West 24th Street New York 10 Telephone Watkins 9-6290
Metro Typographers Incorporated 27 West 24th Street New York 10 Telephone Watkins 9-6290
Metro Typographers Incorporated 27 West 24th Street New York 10 Telephone Watkins 9-6290
Metro Typographers Incorporated 27 West 24th Street New York 10 Telephone Watkins 9-6290
Metro Typographers Incorporated 27 West 24th Street New York 10 Telephone Watkins 9-6290
Metro Typographers Incorporated 27 West 24th Street New York 10 Telephone Watkins 9-6290
Metro Typographers Incorporated 27 West 24th Street New York 10 Telephone Watkins 9-6290
Metro Typographers Incorporated 27 West 24th Street New York 10 Telephone Watkins 9-6290
Metro Typographers Incorporated 27 West 24th Street New York 10 Telephone Watkins 9-6290
Metro Typographers Incorporated 27 West 24th Street New York 10 Telephone Watkins 9-6290
Metro Typographers Incorporated 27 West 24th Street New York 10 Telephone Watkins 9-6290
Metro Typographers Incorporated 27 West 24th Street New York 10 Telephone Watkins 9-6290
Metro Typographers Incorporated 27 West 24th Street New York 10 Telephone Watkins 9-6290
Metro Typographers Incorporated 27 West 24th Street New York 10 Telephone Watkins 9-6290
Metro Typographers Incorporated 27 West 24th Street New York 10 Telephone Watkins 9-6290
Metro Typographers Incorporated 27 West 24th Street New York 10 Telephone Watkins 9-6290
Metro Typographers Incorporated 27 West 24th Street New York 10 Telephone Watkins 9-6290
Metro Typographers Incorporated 27 West 24th Street New York 10 Telephone Watkins 9-6290
Metro Typographers Incorporated 27 West 24th Street New York 10 Telephone Watkins 9-6290
Metro Typographers Incorporated 27 West 24th Street New York 10 Telephone Watkins 9-6290
Metro Typographers Incorporated 27 West 24th Street New York 10 Telephone Watkins 9-6290
Metro Typographers Incorporated 27 West 24th Street New York 10 Telephone Watkins 9-6290
Metro Typographers Incorporated 27 West 24th Street New York 10 Telephone Watkins 9-6290
Metro Typographers Incorporated 27 West 24th Street New York 10 Telephone Watkins 9-6290
Metro Typographers Incorporated 27 West 24th Street New York 10 Telephone Watkins 9-6290
Metro Typographers Incorporated 27 West 24th Street New York 10 Telephone Watkins 9-6290
Metro Typographers Incorporated 27 West 24th Street New York 10 Telephone Watkins 9-6290

MODERN BANKING IS ELECTRONIC BANKING

Technology versus creativity

Considering the technical limitations during the early stages of digital typography, modern enthusiasm for computer technologies may seem surprising. The combination of photography and the drawing board certainly allowed more control over the aesthetic outcome, but control was not necessarily what all designers were after. The new generation of typographers sought new means of expression, which reflected the rebellious spirit of the time. These new means of expression, which were often attributed to the new technology, were neither truly new, nor due to the computer. Phototypesetting, letterpress technology, photography and the photocopier had already been thoroughly exploited for the production of experimental graphics and pre-digital technologies had sufficiently lent themselves to the creation of unexpected results. Due to the largely unknown characteristics of computer technology, the experimental, if not accidental, outcome was now simply closer at hand.

Transitron Electronics and Metro Typographers –
Chermayeff & Geismar
This magazine advert for Transitron Electronics (above) was created using the fragmenting effect of a photographic lens placed on top of the text. The advert for a Typesetting House in New York (opposite) demonstrates how an unusual combination of typefaces turns text into texture.

Show of Force – Chermayeff & Geismar
Chermayeff & Geismar remain active and still produce highly
innovative design solutions. The *Show of Force* identity,
which Chermayeff & Geismar created for a television
production company, proves that this well-established design
agency has learned to apply its creative skills to transitional
media.

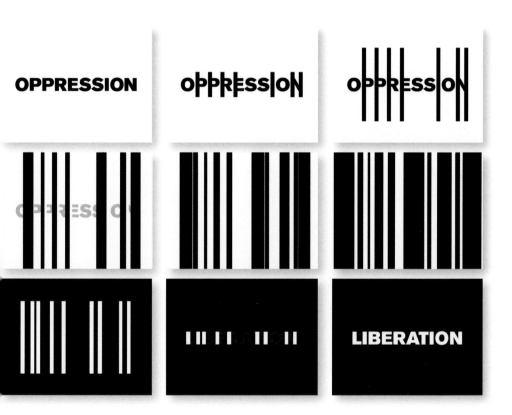

Amnesty International 'Liberation' campaign –
Chermayeff & Geismar

Chermayeff & Geismar's motion graphics for Amnesty International reveal how a simple line pattern can be used effectively to create graphic transitions from one word to the next. As the use of media technologies changes constantly in the context of visual communication, designers need to continuously adapt their principles to evolving means of expression.

Despite the critique of modernists, who feared a decline in typographic standards, a lot of designers embraced computers with an unprecedented degree of enthusiasm. A sometimes joyful, but mostly harsh, representation of contents was the result. Even though the first examples of digital artwork relied on pixel patterns and geometric angles, they were in their playfulness similar to 1970s punk graphics. These punk graphics were, not unlike Dadaism (see pages 18–21 and 62–63), a kind of anti-art, an opposition of the aesthetic principles of the time. Postmodern typographers broke with the established principles in the 1980s. They expressed their rebellious attitude through breaking up the rectangular grid and prioritising individualistic expression over legibility and clarity.

'We argued that there was no such thing as neutrality or transparency in design, that all graphic gestures are loaded with meaning. Also, we weren't interested in addressing the needs of multi-national corporations and lowest common denominator audiences. We were looking to work for smaller cultural institutions and audiences who would enjoy reading visually sophisticated messages.'
<u>Rudy Vanderlans</u>

As Wolfgang Weingart was one of the first design lecturers to apply a more inventive and liberal approach to modernist principles at the art school in Basel, Switzerland, some postmoderninsts used the term 'Swiss Punk' in reference to their work. This typographic label was somewhat misleading because Weingart's reformed idea of modernism had little to do with computer graphics or punk. What Weingart introduced to modernist graphic design in Switzerland from 1968 onwards was a very methodical, hands-on approach to using graphic and photographic textures, as well as typographic structures, to overcome the formal aesthetic restrictions of late modernist designs. Like artist Dieter Roth, Weingart used graphic masks and photographic means to translate type into abstract imagery.

'Pacific Wave' can be seen as a derivative of Weingart's experimental approach. This term, which outlined postmodern typography on the west coast of the United States, was also often misused as an excuse to justify a random approach to typography and graphic layout.

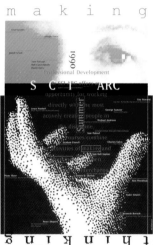

Sci Arc: summer programmes poster and Sci Arc:
making/thinking poster – April Greiman

The origins of the Pacific Wave movement are usually
attributed to April Greiman, a pioneer in computer graphics
and self-acclaimed 'Queen of Chance' (Greiman, 1998).
Greiman trained under Wolfgang Weingart's guidance at
the art school in Basel. As rebellious as Greiman's work
may appear when seen at a glance, her approach to design
had little to do with punk. Weingart's teaching had triggered
Greiman's curiosity about design processes and visual
experimentation. Computer technologies were simply
another means for Greiman to explore the image potential
of typography.

While a lot of other designers used the term 'Pacific Wave'
as an excuse to reject conventions of all kinds, Greiman's
work reveals under close examination that she understood
modernist design principles extremely well. Despite her
vibrant aesthetics, we can see column grids, well-chosen
fonts and carefully adjusted leading and kerning. Greiman
coined the term 'hybrid imagery' for her multi-faceted
digital compositions. Her fusion of text and image produced
colourful, collage-like layouts. Greiman's defiance in using
the rectangle reminds us of futurist works of the early 1920s.
But it was not the pace of life of the industrial age that was
on display here; it was and still is the variety of possibilities
provided by the digital technologies of the time.

matrix

Emperor

OAKLAND

Emigre

Matrix, Emperor, Oakland and Emigre – Zuzana Licko
In retrospect, technical possibilities have not always
been quite as generous as postmodernist design solutions
suggest. These graphics were often the result of a tough
battle against the much restricted processing power of
the first generations of Macintosh computers. Some type
designs such as Zuzana Licko's Matrix from 1986 showed
how the design of vector-based PostScript fonts could be
tailored towards the low-memory capacities of the early
128K Macs. Other fonts, including Licko's Oakland, Emigre
and Emperor from 1985, could be seen as a tribute to
the technological limitations of the early stages of
digital typography.

In Matrix, Licko defined the shape of the individual letters
according to the number of pixels used vertically by the
upper case letters. This resulted in a variety of versions
for each font, all of which were dependent on type size
and named in accordance to their pixel resolution.

Emigre magazine – Rudy Vanderlans, Menno Meyjes, Marc Susan
Since 1983 Zuzana Licko has been married to Rudy Vanderlans, who launched *Emigre* magazine together with Menno Meyjes and Marc Susan in 1984. The publication was subtitled, 'The magazine that ignores boundaries', but rather than ignoring the boundaries or limits of digital technologies, *Emigre* placed them at the centre of attention. By combining conventional methods of reproduction such as Xerox and letterpress technology with computer graphics and digital typography, *Emigre* showcased the limited possibilities of the early Macintosh computers. The magazine also reinforced the then-current fascination with the potential future significance of digital technologies. Thus, *Emigre* remained one of the most influential design magazines until the last issue was published in 2005. Even though only a few copies of *Emigre* magazine remain available, Emigre Inc. continues to trade typefaces.

By the time computers emerged, modern typography already had a long-lasting tradition in Europe. As European designers were more conscious of modernist principles, the revolution was a little more moderate in comparison to the new trends in the United States. Rule books were reviewed rather than rejected. Questions were raised and discussed, but remained often unresolved. Interesting developments happened within the dialectic tension between modernism and postmodernism, in particular with regard to the relationship between image and text.

'Design, of course, is also a form of expression, but expression as a by-product of the process rather than self-expression as a goal in itself...'
Simon Johnston

Haçienda – 8vo

8vo was a London design group founded by Mark Holt and
Simon Johnston in 1984. Hamish Muir joined in 1985 and
Michael Burke in 1986. Both Muir and Johnston had studied
under Wolfgang Weingart in Basel and all four members of
the group shared the belief that typography could be at the
core of graphic design solutions.

8vo's work shows that the computer was not always
essential to produce highly sophisticated design solutions
in the 1980s. No matter how complex their final pieces,
their designs were initially drawn by hand and mocked-up
with great care and attention to detail. While magazines
used a mark-up grid, the type used for posters could be
treated more flexibly. The initial layout sketches were refined,
coloured and finalised in stages. In 1986 Tony Wilson
from Factory Records commissioned 8vo to develop this
fourth anniversary poster for the Manchester nightclub, the
Haçienda. This series of images shows the enormous manual
effort behind the finished poster.

④ Digital typography: 4.3 New trends in Europe

4.2 Swiss Punk and the Pacific Wave ⟵ ⟶ 4.4 Technology and beyond

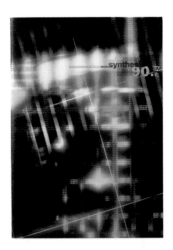

<u>Octavo</u> 92.8 – 8vo

The last issue of *Octavo* deserves some special attention. It was the only *Octavo* issue to be developed using a computer. It also came in the form of an interactive CD-ROM, a communication device that was still in the early stages of development in 1992. The unusual format of issue 92.8 reinforced the challenging questions raised about the future of typography in the context of digital communication. The fact that some of these questions still remain unanswered shows us how profound the impact of digital technology was at the time.

'...digital technologies are never around for long enough for us to build a true understanding of their nature.'
<u>Jon Wozencroft</u>

In order to express their views, and those of their peers, 8vo created a multi-linear narrative. By clicking on key words, the user could decide on the order of the text contents. Spoken texts were then disclosed in combination with displayed text elements. The user pressed the period or the comma signs to continue the text display. By fragmenting the sentences, 8vo forced the user to pause, inviting them to reflect on certain text content a little while longer. These pauses, which we experience naturally during verbal conversations, are now almost lost in the context of digital typography. It suggests that 8vo sensed the need to pace carefully the transmission of digital text information.

'We tried not to have a style, but an approach, a method of working.'
<u>Simon Johnston</u>

Fuse magazine

Fuse was a magazine designed by Neville Brody and written by Jon Wozencroft that aimed to widen the context within which typography was discussed in the early 1990s. The contents of the 20 different *Fuse* issues was arranged in a systematic order to discuss the cultural and technological progression of written languages. To achieve a conclusive judgment on the relevance of typography it is generally insufficient to discuss the zeitgeist – the spirit of the age – of a particular point in time. To tackle this problem, *Fuse* discussed typography as a dynamic cultural product that responds to, as much as it evolves from, social, cultural, and technological developments. Various *Fuse* issues indicated that the subject of virtual typography is by no means restricted to postmodernist styles or technological achievements. Virtual typography may likewise be related to the roots of writing such as hieroglyphs and runes as well as to other forms of linguistic codes such as Braille and Morse.

Fuse Fonts

Fuse Fonts is a range of typefaces that evolved alongside *Fuse* magazine. After fonts and layouts had suffered from the technological restrictions of the first generations of Macintosh computers, as well as from the early versions of design and font-editing software, typographers could challenge the pixel aesthetics of low-resolution computer graphics in the early 1990s.

FF Moonbase Alpha and FF Dot Matrix – Cornel Windlin
Cornel Windlin is a designer and art director from Zurich, Switzerland. Windlin began to work on his typeface FF Moonbase Alpha (above left) in 1990. This type design responded to the rough-edged looks of early computer graphics by softening the contours of the pixel-based letter shapes. The low-resolution rendering of a font in Photoshop, followed by the increase in image size and contrast, proved to be a reliable means of introducing a more organic feel to digital typography.

When designing his FF Dot Matrix (above right), Windlin thoroughly explored the printing technologies of the time. He examined everything from supermarket checkout tills to ticket vending machines. FF Dot Matrix was inspired by dot matrix printers.

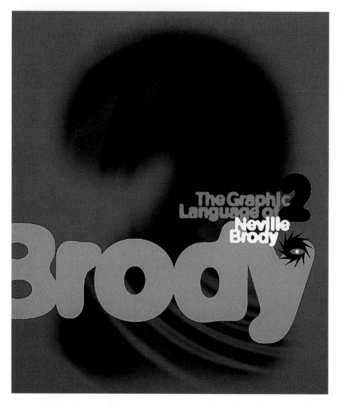

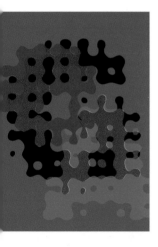

DIGITALOGUE

<u>Various works</u> – Neville Brody

Brody's career as a designer was jump-started only two years after completing his studies at the London College of Printing (now London College of Communication), when he became art director of the British fashion magazine *The Face* in 1981. Like much of his early work, type and layout were defined here through sharp angles and geometric shapes.

Brody's design of the 'Astropolis' logo (opposite, above left) for the cover of a book by Taruho Inagaki in 1991 still reflects these aesthetic principles.

At the turn of the decade Brody's design began to change significantly. Shapes became softer, contours sometimes blurred, and overlapping elements often remained translucent. Brody's font FF Blur (opposite, above right), which characterises the cover of Jon Wozencroft's second volume of *The Graphic Language of Neville Brody* (opposite, bottom left), illustrates this change in direction.

Brody's exploration of visually challenging type was taken further when he reversed FF Blur to create the poster Autosuggestion (opposite, bottom right) for *Fuse* issue 9. Here, reading is turned into a guessing game even for the visually trained eye.

This attempt to communicate on the borderline of legibility was taken even further when Brody developed the brand identity for Digitalogue (this page, left), a Japanese CD-ROM publisher, in 1992. Here Brody manipulated ink blobs to make each letter appear like a liquid shape. Where the letters overlap the visual turns into a colourful chaos. Only when seen next to one another can the letter shapes be recognised as typographic symbols.

FF Virtual (this page, above), a font Brody designed for *Fuse* issue 5, is completely illegible. The dot pattern in some of the letters such as the upper case 'A' reminds the viewer of Braille. The lower case shown here in red is simply the reversal of the upper case printed in dark grey. The black glyphs are the numbers 1 to 9 with 0 at the end.

As soon as initial problems with the availability and compatibility of digital equipment were overcome, computer-based typography offered technically perfect results. The precision with which computers calculated typographic compositions put all previous technologies such as phototypesetting in the shade. But some designers considered the technical perfection to be another challenge to be tackled. They strove for diversity and individuality, finding the clean-cut results of computer-generated typefaces too cold and impersonal.

'I am really interested in type that isn't perfect, type that reflects more truly the imperfect language of an imperfect world inhabited by imperfect beings.'
Barry Deck

Fontographer

The international distribution of Fontographer, a type-design software originally developed by Altsys in 1985, lead to a boom in typeface design in the late 1980s. Thanks to software developments, and technologies allowing the online distribution of fonts, the DIY attitude that had been seen during the 1970s punk period was re-introduced to typography. The ease with which fonts could be copied without purchasing licenses lead to a situation where designers often ended up with huge collections of fonts.

'Technology is nothing more than a process, not an end in itself.'
Jonathan Barnbrook

Beowolf and Trixie – LettError

LettError was the title of a typographic joint project between Erik van Blokland and Just van Rossum, who both worked for the renowned design office MetaDesign in Berlin. The Dutch design duo understood programming well enough to make deliberate use of pre-programmed computational errors for aesthetic purposes. Their typeface Beowolf (opposite, top two images) (1989), uses a code that moves corner points randomly along the outline. This causes an alteration in shape each time a letter is printed. This computational inconsistency defied the digital perfectionism even more than Trixie (opposite, bottom image), a font that had been created in 1991 on the basis of the type of an old typewriter, and named after a friend, Beatrix, who owned the machine, even though there is not a single point left in the font that relates to the original machine. Trixie and Beowolf can be seen as a reaction against the clinical perfection of computer technology.

The Desperate **Chainsaws**
19: Open Mike Night* (A)
20: NoMoreCurves (UK)
+ Bassment (Amsterdam)
21: Urban Death Ray (D)
Assinine Megaturbidites
22. Sedimäntary Bodeez

Beowolf

Beowolf

Beowolf

tromeganiese-, of el
waarmee skryftekens
Български: Пишеща м
натискане на клавиши
Пишещите машини са м
Català. Màquina d'e
rell mecànic, electr
cles que en ser pres

'Scratchiness is intentionally
misaligned and almost
purposefully sloppy – a celebration
of all that is ill-resolved and
non-committal.'
Jessica Helfand

Typographic designer David Carson sparked what Jessica Helfand coined the 'cult of the scratchy'. This was another trend that raised questions about the relevance of legibility in relation to typographic forms of expression. But the 'cult of the scratchy' did not follow any rationale. In order to avoid the need for intellectual justification, Kerrie Jacobs took refuge by referring to intuitive design practice in her introduction to Carson's second book *2nd Sight*. But is it so unthinkable to assess analytically the role of intuition in the context of communication? The philosopher Nelson Goodman suggests that 'in aesthetic experience emotions function cognitively' (Nelson, 1969). The aesthetics of typographic work communicate by provoking emotive responses.

Emotional stimulation – as difficult as it may be to explain – is relevant to the communication process. But as designers do not tend to read philosophy, critical discourse did not survive throughout the 1990s, and the digital revolution in typography started to run out of steam. Even where designers were not forced to sacrifice their stylistic ambitions to the demands of the mainstream market, postmodernism had been absorbed by the industries that welcomed the emotive qualities of postmodern typography. All that was left was the debate that juxtaposed the slogans 'form follows function' and 'form follows fun'.

RayGun – David Carson
David Carson's success in the 1990s nourished the belief of many that anyone could become a typographer. Having never had a formal design education, Carson tried his hand at the design of various magazines including *Beach Culture* until he managed to leave his mark on typography with his work for *RayGun*. Now the spirit of punk graphics had returned once again, if only aesthetically. But Carson's grungy, Generation-X-based agitation seemed devoid of any message or agenda that would go beyond the notion that there is more to culture than the mainstream. As much as Dadaism was anti-art, Carson's version of postmodern typography was a kind of anti-design, an empty message to ridicule the design establishment.

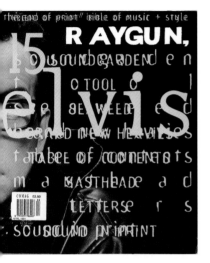

Film title sequences

Film title sequences can be seen as the origin of motion graphics and of transitional typography. However, film titles initially consisted of static title cards only. In silent cinema, title cards also helped to convey dialogues. The introduction of sound brought little improvement to the basic treatment of text information. Only when films were distributed in colour, towards the end of the 1950s, were film titles given more attention. During the 1960s various graphic designers, including Maurice Binder and Pablo Ferro, thrived on the challenge of packaging films. A new genre of graphic communication was born.

Se7en film title – Imaginary Forces

Kyle Cooper co-founded Imaginary Forces, one of the world's most prominent film design companies. Having directed over 150 film title sequences, Cooper managed to draw attention to the genre of film title design like nobody else since Saul Bass in the 1950s and Pablo Ferro in the 1960s. With his title sequence for *Se7en* in 1995, Kyle Cooper effectively applied 'scratchy' aesthetics to motion graphics. Cooper drew text information directly on to the film material. On the celluloid, the ink could easily be manipulated. By pasting the results on to a seemingly random collage of background imagery, Cooper gave the title sequence a scrappy, handmade look. Some of Cooper's first independent title sequences followed a similar stylist approach. What prevails in his later work is his insatiable curiosity about new ways of typographic manipulation. In 2003, Cooper moved on to create Prologue Films, another film design company of international repute.

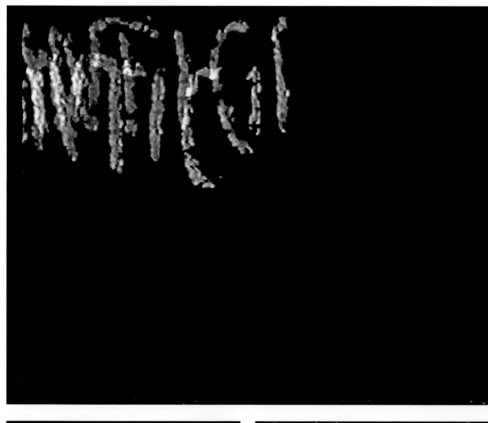

Anticipation of the Night – Stan Brakhage

Kyle Cooper was not the first to explore the technique of drawing directly on to film before processing it. Stan Brakhage exploited this technique for the title of his experimental film *Anticipation of the Night* (1962). The avant-garde filmmaker introduced many inspiring ways of manipulating film material. By working directly on filmstrips, sometimes without even using any camera equipment whatsoever, Brakhage produced results that raised questions about the very nature of film. Even though the latest software technology allows simulation of some of those film manipulation techniques, the digitisation of film editing appears to have weakened our awareness for the true potential of conventional media technologies. The solarisation filter, offered as part of the drop-down menu of our software applications, for example, hardly reflects the way the intermediate exposure of film materials in the dark room modifies the end result of photographic processing.

Hard- and software developments did not only stimulate designers' interest in type design, it also allowed them to approach media other than print. The Internet spread quickly across the world in the mid-1990s and lead to a boom in interactive design. Motion graphics software applications invited graphic designers to enter the genre of film title design and television advertising. A multidisciplinary approach to design became popular amongst design collectives who could share the diversity of their specialist skills to cover a wide range of tasks.

Television identities

The Internet offers limited scope for the display of transitional typography. Although websites consist of largely static 'pages', the perception of information is discontinuous. As the reader determines the order in which information is perceived, the information appears fragmented. The vast amount of information on offer induces users to click through information fast, which often leads to a sense of impatience. Televised information is also increasingly fragmented and subject to acceleration. The more information is required to suit the concept of time–space compression in order to remain economically viable, the less room there is for gradually unfolding forms of typographic expression. The area of television identities is probably the most likely to accommodate time-based typography, as here the television channels are free to decide on their own time slots.

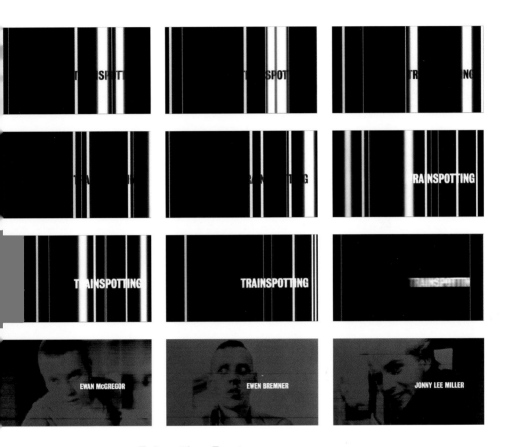

Trainspotting – Tomato

Tomato was founded in 1991 as a collective of artists, designers, musicians and writers. A commission to produce the music, titles and closing sequence for the film *Trainspotting* in 1996 put them firmly on the map of the international graphic design scene. Jason Kedgley and Dylan Kendle animated textures of lines that simultaneously symbolise the passing of train coaches and the tracks of needles on human skin. Their motion graphic also symbolises the intertwining of the protaganists' stories.

The animation was originally created in Macromedia Director, a multimedia design software, and printed frame by frame before being copied with a thermographic fax. Each fax frame was then 'rostrummed' sequentially, which produced the right look and texture, but did not provide consistent results. This affected legibility of the type and also made frame registration impossible. So Kedgley and Kendle abandoned their first attempt and decided to recreate the animation in an online suite. But the brown and cream colouring of the visuals that was meant to hint at heroin consumption got lost in transition to digital. The remnants of the first approach can be seen in these character cards (shown at the end of the film as thermofacsimiles of photographs).

Profile – Why Not Associates

This design group was founded by Andrew Altmann, David Ellis and Howard Greenhalgh in London in 1987. Their television title sequence *Profile* illustrates well how motion graphics allow for the delay of the communication of text, because they intensify the visual tension that keeps viewers in suspense. The animation, produced for BBC4 in 2002, uses the rotary motion of typographic fragments to achieve its visually intriguing effect. The time-based disposition of typographic elements was achieved through the use of a filter in Adobe After Effects. Visual effects, which are part of the software used, are always restricted by the number of parameters the software application has to offer. They are also likely to be copied by other designers. Nevertheless this example retains its remarkable quality.

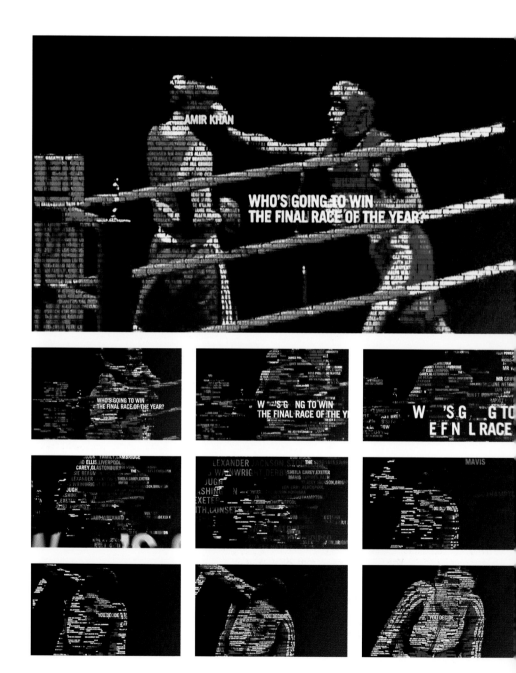

④ **Digital typography:** 4.6 Multidisciplinary design
4.5 The 'cult of the scratchy' ← → 4.7 Coded typography

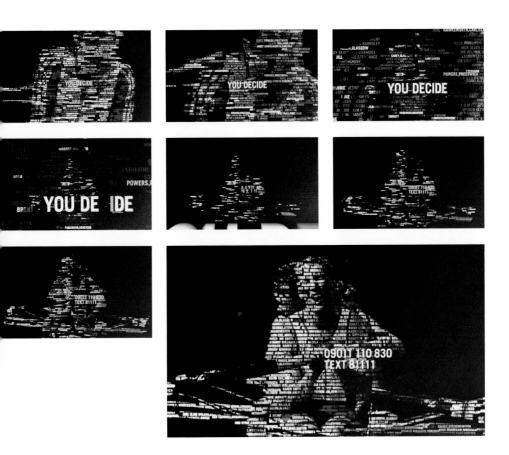

BBC Sports Personality of the Year – Why Not Associates

Why Not Associates' promotional clip for the *BBC Sports Personality of the Year* programme, from 2004, was a larger commission that allowed the design group an even more sophisticated approach. This example is particularly interesting with regard to the dynamic relationship between image and text, because it uses a zoom effect in combination with typographic textures to blend one moving image sequence into the next. The imagery seems to fall apart into the fragments of a text, so the balance shifts from image to text and back to the next image.

Pobl and Machines – Why Not Associates

The company's portfolio is still expanding into new areas. The collaboration with artist Gordon Young helped Why Not Associates to produce work that sits on the borderline between sculptural art and communication design. _Pobl_ is the Welsh word for 'people'. _Pobl and machines_ is a row of letter-shaped seats situated in front of the National Waterfront Museum in Swansea, Wales. Each letter represents an item that can be found inside the museum.

<u>Blackpool climbing towers</u> – Why Not Associates
Another project concept by Gordon Young was the design of two 20-metre-high climbing towers, created for Blackpool Council in England in 2006. The towers were cast in black concrete. White granite inserts emphasise this gigantic piece of typography. Each face of the two towers offers climbing routes of different levels of difficulty.

Digital typography does not necessarily require fonts and computer software applications. Type can also be constructed from simple graphic shapes, which can be defined through hard coding. Hard coding is the manipulation of the source code of a computer program. While graphic designers commonly use existing software applications for the development of their designs, programmers use 'programming environments' to define the solutions via programming languages such as Perl, C++ or Java (not to be confused with JavaScript). In the mid-1990s, when most graphic designers could only expand on the growing number of Photoshop layers or on the 3D plug-ins of their illustration software, John Maeda, who was at the time Professor of Media Arts and Sciences at MIT, promoted the concept of creating typographic solutions through hard coding. Programmers began to enter the arena of typographic design.

Coded variety
Whereas graphic designers are often worried about becoming slaves to their tools when using predefined software features, programmers are able to develop their tools from scratch. But programming methods for creating type are mostly examined on the basis of what is technically possible, and not in response to what forms of typographic expression would be needed to communicate effectively within digital environments. This is why many of the highly innovative ideas do not receive the attention they deserve in the public domain. What seems crucial is the way in which typographic information is perceived. Therefore, the following chapter will discuss the process of reading, the understanding of which will allow us to evaluate better transitional typography in the context of visual communication.

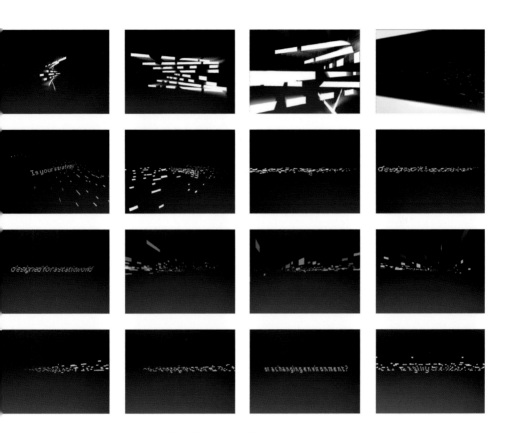

Questions – Imaginary Forces

Peter Cho is a Los Angeles-based media artist and designer who holds a Master of Science degree from the MIT Media Lab, and a Master of Fine Arts degree from the University of California, Los Angeles (UCLA) Design/Media Arts department. This typographic animation created by Cho for IBM, under the creative direction of Mikon van Gastel at Imaginary Forces, shows visual effects similar to those used by Why Not Associates for the _Profiles_ animation (see page 106). Rotating typographic elements merge over a period of time to turn into words. Cho coded his solution based on Open GL and C++, which allowed him a far greater flexibility in the variation of the typographic transitions. Cho's motion graphics show how virtual typography can operate rhythmically. If transitions between image and text patterns are repeated systematically, virtual typography stimulates the viewer's mind due to its transitional characteristics as well as the viewer's expectation of recurring patterns. While one word takes shape, is read and reflected upon, another one emerges so that the momentum is sustained. The intellectual reflection that follows the cognitive phase is accompanied by the next phase of aesthetic stimulation. Cho manages to find a perfect balance between the continuity of motion and the variation in transition.

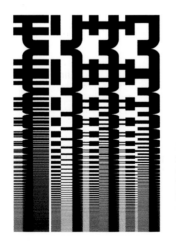

❹ **Digital typography:** 4.7 Coded typography
4.6 Multidisciplinary design ←

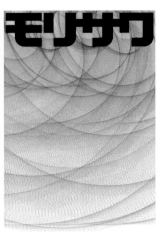

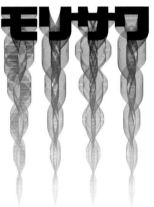

*'Every form is but the external
expression of its internal function.
Form and function are, ultimately,
related to each other dialectically.'*
Dr Kim Young-Oak

Morisawa – John Maeda

Maeda's poster designs for the Japanese type foundry
Morisawa illustrate the versatility of a programming-based
approach to typography. Changing the parameters in the
source code allows for an unlimited amount of variations in
the typographic transformations, which are here frozen on
to paper. Kim Young-Oak, a Korean philosopher, playwright
and medical doctor, describes the beauty in nature as 'that-
which-is-so-to-itself'. According to Young-Oak, 'Nature's
function does not decorate itself'. John Maeda's work is
fascinating because its complexity seems self-explanatory.
One can easily sense the mathematical rigour behind
Maeda's creations, even if the code remains a puzzling
secret. So his work appears both simple and sophisticated
at the same time.

It is interesting that there was so much debate about the degree to which typography should be legible in the 1990s despite the fact that we did not even know exactly how written text is perceived by the reader. Various hypotheses have been developed but scientists still cannot agree which one to trust. The problem is that it is impossible to establish hard evidence for the process of reading. All that can be examined scientifically is the cognition of written words and letters but not how the human brain assembles words and letters to construct meaning. This chapter looks into some of the existing theories, all of which indicate that reading results from a process of speculation. Both the cognition of text elements and the intellectual determination of text contents follow a process of continuous hypothesis testing. This process, which evidently applies to static text, will also reveal why gradually evolving typography is so visually compelling.

Read On – Typeworkshop
Typeworkshop evolved from a range of workshops given by Underware in various countries (see also <www.typeworkshop. com>). Underware, a graphic design studio founded by Akiem Helmling, Bas Jacobs and Sami Kortemäki in the Netherlands in 1999, specialises in the design and production of typefaces. It is interesting to see that the participants of the Read On workshop, which took place in Lausanne in 2005, chose books to spell the word 'Liberté', symbolising the knowledge and understanding spread through the written word that liberates societies from oppression of aristocratic and clerical leadership. Now there seems to be a shift back to the use of images and icons in the context of visual communication, and advertisers and corporations well understand how to exploit this trend to increase their control over people.

The Bouma theory assumes that text is perceived word by word rather than letter by letter. Its supporters claim that readers perceive words as clusters of letters, similar to logotypes, which communicate through their overall shape and outline rather than through their precise spelling. The Bouma model evolved from evidence that was gathered in the field of cognitive psychology since the 1970s. Contemporary psychologists use the word 'Bouma' synonymously with 'word shape' in tribute to Herman Bouma, who discussed the concept in his paper 'Visual Interference in the Parafoveal Recognition of Initial and Final Letters of Words' in 1973. The fovea is the location at the back of the eye that allows us to depict objects in detail. Surrounding the fovea is the parafoveal area that is responsible for our peripheral vision. Herman Bouma claimed that readers look at the centre of a word while they recognise the surrounding letters using their peripheral vision.

James Cattel is considered by many to be the first psychologist to propose (in 1886) that reading results from the recognition of complete words rather than individual letters. The Bouma theory is supported by the fact that spelling mistakes are missed significantly more often where the shape of the incorrect word is consistent with that of the correct word. On the other hand, the idea of reading words on the basis of either their outlines or their rhythm of ascending and descending letters has raised doubts because the outline of words, as well as the rhythm of ascending and descending letters, are evidently not sufficient for the recognition of words. But the Bouma theory also relies on other criteria such as word boundaries, which are determined by the blank space between words, the frequency of words within a text, as well as consistency in the linguistic structure of phrases (for example, subject-verb-object). So the hypothesis retains much of its credibility.

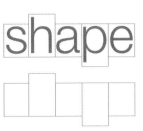 

Bouma shapes

Bouma shapes based on ascending and descending letters (above left), and Bouma shapes based on the word envelope (above right), as illustrated in *Typo*, January 2005.

Target word: **test**	Error rate
Consistent word shape **(tesf)**	13%
Consistent word shape **(tesc)**	7%

Error rates

Error rates in relation to word shapes: consistency in the word shape makes misreading more likely, as illustrated in *Typo*, January 2005.

⊏⌐ almost every day ⊏⊐ ⊡ large lumber mill. ⊡
liked ⊏⊐ listen ⊏⊐ ⊏⊐ scraping ⊏⌐ grinding ⊏⌐
⊏⊐ machinery ⊏⌐ watch ⊏⊐ ⊏⊐ busy men at work.
⊏⌐ father made ⊡ comfortable little seat ⊏⌐ ⊏⊐.
⊏⊐ ⊡ ⊏⌐ sit and watch ⊏⊐ sharp saw cut through
⊏⊐ big logs, scattering sparks.

Recognition

Neither the outline of words (above left) nor the rhythm of ascending and descending letters (above right) is sufficient for the recognition of words, as illustrated in *Typo*, January 2005.

These two concepts are conflicting theories. They both provide different answers to the question of how texts are scanned. Do people read various letters of a word subsequently or simultaneously?

Serial letter recognition

According to the serial letter recognition theory, words are scanned letter by letter starting with the one that is furthest left. This model is supported by experiments that provide proof that long words require more time to be recognised than short ones. Like the Bouma model, this theory emerged in the early 1970s. However, it was short-lived and was rejected due to the so-called 'word superiority effect', which revealed that letters are more easily identified as part of a word than in isolation.

Parallel letter recognition

The parallel letter recognition theory, developed in 1989, is the most recent model and remains the most popular. This theory assumes that all the letters of a word are registered simultaneously and analysed in conjunction. The ability to perceive various letters simultaneously is apparently aided by the foveal recognition mentioned earlier. Foveal recognition means that objects that are just outside people's optical focal point are still registered, though not as clearly as the object in focus. We experience this when we detect moving objects out of the corner of our eyes. The foveal area is particularly sensitive to motion – a fact that is worth bearing in mind, because it allows the designer of motion graphics to guide the viewer's focus of attention.

chart	Identical word (control)	210ms
chovt	Similar word shape Some letters in common	240ms
chyft	Dissimilar word shape Some letters in common	280ms
ebovf	Similar word shape No letters in common	300ms

Relative speed of boundary (in milliseconds)
Words which are misspelled in the beginning of the word take longer to be deciphered than words with spelling mistakes at the end of the word. Does this prove that people read letter by letter from left to right? As illustrated in *Typo*, January 2005.

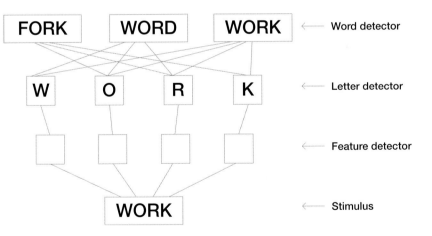

Parallel letter recognition
The principle of parallel letter recognition, according to which letters are analysed individually but simultaneously, as illustrated in *Typo*, January 2005.

Both the Bouma hypothesis and the parallel letter recognition theory are supported by the discovery of saccadic eye movement. It has been known since the late nineteenth century that the scanning of text does not follow a smooth pattern. But where the eyes come to a halt and how long they rest on certain points remained unclear for many decades. Precise evidence for the quick and unconscious eye movement involved in reading – the 'saccades' – could only be established thanks to the increasing accuracy of eye-tracking technologies, which now allow us to measure and monitor the motion of the reader's eyes with great precision. Now we know for certain that human eyes jump from word to word, sometimes from syllable to syllable, rather than from letter to letter. The fixation period is the time span during which the eyes do not move. Fixation spans constitute an interruption of the scanning process and provide important evidence on how text is perceived. Whilst words are fixated for 200–250 milliseconds, the jumps of the reader's eyes between words (the saccades) take only about 20–35 milliseconds. Whether the Bouma model deserves more credibility than the parallel letter recognition theory or vice versa, or if a combination of both models would be most appropriate, remains a highly contentious issue. Either way, people read word by word.

Intelligent guesswork

Curiously, words are not necessarily fixated in the order of their occurrence. Ten to 15 per cent of all saccades are regressive. This means that the eyes jump frequently backwards in a sentence during the reading process. Equally important is the fact that the forward saccades often skip one or several words. This indicates that reading is a matter of hypothesis testing. Readers seem to make assumptions about unseen text elements in order to skip certain words and to be able to read more quickly. The regressive saccades suggest that readers sometimes need to verify the assumptions made by jumping backwards, so as to double-check the meaning of certain words which were skipped at first. It seems evident that the scanning pattern of the reader's eyes depends on his or her expectations of the text content that is to yet come. This process of hypothesis testing applies to virtual typography too. As soon as a graphic pattern starts to take on typographic characteristics, expectations of emerging text information arise. The viewer then tries to assemble the graphic elements in his or her mind like the pieces of a puzzle.

Roadside joggers endure sweat, pain and angry drivers in

the name of fitness. A healthy body may seem reward...

Saccadic eye movements
As illustrated in *Typo*, January 2005.

As mentioned previously, reading goes well beyond the cognitive processing dimension. Whether or not a reader understands what is written depends on the context as well as on their interpretative capability. Memorisation of the text content much depends on the degree to which the reader enjoys the reading process.

The reader-response theory

In order to examine both the interpretation of text as well as the joy that accompanies it, **Wolfgang Iser** developed the so-called 'reader-response theory'. This theory bears some similarities to the principle of saccadic perception but it goes beyond the structure of individual sentences, as it extends the idea of hypothesis testing beyond the cognitive phase to the interpretative capacity of the reader. Iser asserts that each sentence contains hints of the following one, calling those hints 'semantic pointers'. These semantic pointers provoke the reader to make assumptions about what is going to be said in the sentences to come. As the reader's expectations depend on his or her personal knowledge and experience, every reader interprets a sentence slightly differently. Reading is therefore not a passive, one-way process. It also depends on the reader, who must use his or her imagination to reconstruct meaning. Interestingly, Iser believes the joy of reading to be rooted precisely in this productive, proactive, contribution by the reader.

The wandering viewpoint

Where the reader takes on an active role in the determination of the significance of a message, and be it just to some degree, it is no longer the text that dominates the reader's thoughts. The reader's thoughts in return modify the meaning of the text. Reading is subjective because meaning depends on the reader's individual expectations, interests and understanding. Of course the author can tailor his or her writing towards

Wolfgang Iser

Wolfgang Iser (1926–2007) was a German literary scholar and professor of English and comparative literature at the University of Constance. He co-founded the Constance School of Reception Aesthetics, which dates back to the late 1960s. In his book *The Act of Reading* (1978), Iser shifts his emphasis from the traditional emphasis on the production of texts to the process of reading in order to analyse the reader's contact with text and the author.

the reader's imagination. Through contradicting or fulfilling the reader's expectations writers can play with the reader's imagination. This indicates that meaning conveyed by text does not reside within the structure of individual sentences, but also in the way the diversity of sentences correlate. Iser refers to changes in the reader's perspective on text contents as the reader's 'wandering viewpoint'. Reading differs from the perception of given objects because 'the whole text can never be perceived at any one time' (Iser, 1978). Words and sentences constitute text fragments that need to be reassembled in the reader's mind. This is why texts communicate in a fundamentally different way to images (which can be viewed at a glance). It also means that the intelligent guesswork mentioned above does not only relate to the recognition of words and sentences but also to their correlative meaning.

'...it is the very lack of control that forms the basis of the creative side of reading.'
Wolfgang Iser

Clock – Christiian Postma
Christiian Postma is a Dutch artist and designer who works
and lives in Stockholm, Sweden. Postma explores 'the
unexpected' and seeks to strike the viewer with surprise.
Following an investigation into time, Postma arranged
more than 150 individual clockworks in systematic order to
produce a clock sized 140cm by 140cm. Postma illustrates
the progression of time by letting numbers gradually
emerge in the shape of written words. Due to the careful
synchronisation of the clockworks, the words 'one' to
'twelve' become readable one by one precisely when they
are needed to indicate the relevant time. So the word 'four'
becomes legible when it is four o'clock and it dissolves again
as time moves on. The word 'five' begins to appear and by
five o'clock the word 'five' is clearly visible, while the word
'four' has already vanished.

*'To define is to kill,
to suggest is to create.'*
<u>Stéphane Mallarmé</u>

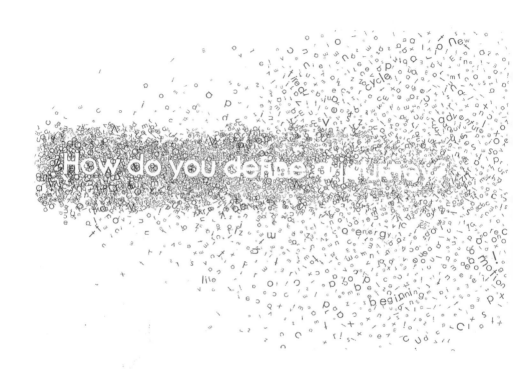

How do you define a journey? – Adam Field
    Adam Field was a student at the London College of
Communication when he created this large-format print.
Field hoped to break down words to allow for multiple
interpretations of his typographic composition. The type
communicates on two layers: the question appears from
the omission of type in certain areas and becomes
increasingly illegible towards the end, yet the seemingly
random letters surrounding the letters that shape the
question invite the reader to search for words within the
chaos of the type. While the words, which evolve from the
gaps between letters, phrase the question, the form of their
visual presentation points towards an answer. A journey
through text defined by chance?

Edmund Husserl

In the context of philosophy
Edmund Husserl (1859–1938)
is seen as the founder of
phenomenology, a branch of
philosophy that considers all
knowledge to be rooted in people's
subjective experience. Many other
philosophers including Heidegger,
Merleau-Ponty, Sartre and Derrida
drew on Husserl's theories. Husserl
taught philosophy at various
universities in Germany until he
retired in Freiburg, where he was
superseded by Martin Heidegger
in 1928.

*'Faced with the beautiful,
analytical reflection restores the
temps durée through the medium
of its antithesis. Analysis
terminates in beauty.'*
Theodor Adorno

Time and tension

As much as one sentence points to the next to come,
it also relates to the expectation triggered by the previous
one. By fulfilling or contradicting the expectations
made, each sentence modifies the understanding of
what was previously said. So the text is constantly
re-evaluated and the reader's memories transformed.
In a wider sense, this process of continuously rethinking
the past and the future reflects the way people perceive
temporal progression in general. According to **Edmund
Husserl**, a German philosopher, the present moment
can only be perceived indirectly through the dialectical
tension between past and future events. In other
words, people develop their awareness of the present
through constantly comparing their expectations of
what is about to happen in the future to that which has
happened. Husserl refers to the anticipation of future
events as 'protensions' and to memorised sensations
as 'retentions'. Like the present moment in real life, the
content of a written text remains constantly dynamic.
Depending on the sequential structure of sentences and
contents, new thoughts are evoked and the reader's
perspective is shifted. The continual interplay between
protensions and retentions can result in a constantly
upheld tension. Following Iser, protensions in the context
of literature should therefore not lead to fulfillment, but
to a succession of protensions. This allows for the
constantly upheld tension that sustains the reader's
interest and perpetuates the joy of reading.

Without understanding people's perception of time, it is difficult to appreciate the benefits of virtual typography. Virtual typography defies the instantaneous presentation of information. Thus it undermines what people frequently refer to as 'real time' in relation to digital communication.

Perceptions of time

Design critic Jessica Helfand declares 'real time' a myth by claiming that in reality, time can take on many forms. The urge for time efficiency is a cultural phenomenon. So is people's dependence on the clock. The degree to which one enjoys a period of time cannot be measured in terms of minutes or seconds. This is where Helfand's notion of 'quality time' comes into play. The fact that the quality of time cannot be measured reminds us of **Henry Bergson**, a French philosopher who proposed to distinguish between time extensity that is marked by the succession of different events, and time intensity, which reflects the degree to which people are immersed in individual events. Bergson claimed that time extensity is an artificial construct that blinds people to the true nature of time, which is in fact continuous and non-fragmented. If people enjoy a period of time they will find the extent of this period difficult to evaluate in terms of the 'amount' of time that is passing by. Time becomes immeasurable.

'From our division of time into uniform, visualizable units comes our sense of duration and our impatience when we cannot endure the delay between events. Such a sense of impatience, or of time as duration, is unknown among non-literate cultures.'
Marshall McLuhan

'...most ironically in our impatient electronic culture, the phrase "Real Time" has come to symbolize the instantaneous, the nanosecond, or, what distinguished media oracle Marshall McLuhan once referred to as "allatonceness". Today, as we struggle to reconcile the virtual against the tangible, what does it mean to be real at all?'
Jessica Helfand

Even though Bergson's point of view has been highly disputed in the course of the twentieth century, we cannot deny the fact that we become oblivious to the amount of time passing by when we are captivated by an experience. If time consciousness is the result of a constant interchange between a perceptual future

'Why is this non-instantaneous time not referred to as reflective time? Or thoughtful time? Or quality time?'
Jessica Helfand

(protension) and a perceptual past (retention), we may also assume that the more intensively we focus on either the future or the past, the less conscious we are of the quantifiable progression of time.

Virtual typography makes people experience time as intensive because it imposes a state of confusion. While the continuity of transformation makes viewers concentrate on the future (when trying to predict the emerging shape of the anticipated text information), it also requires the constant evaluation of the present data by comparing it to what was seen so far (does any of the data resemble anything ever seen before?). If the viewer's time consciousness fluctuates between past and future, their awareness of the present moment is weakened and their focus of attention is sustained.

....

Henry Bergson

....

Bergson (1859–1941) was a French philosopher who argued in favour of intuition over intellect. His speculative thoughts on the nature of time have influenced many other philosophers and writers including Gilles Deleuze's analysis of the 'movement-image' and the 'time image'. Bergson was awarded the Nobel Prize for Literature in 1927.

Virtual typography exists prior to the manifestation of a linguistic code; before it turns into 'actual' typography it cannot transport any literal meaning.

'The wandering viewpoint'

The display of seemingly typographic patterns in the context of transitional typography triggers expectations within the viewer. Depending on the continuing transition of the pattern, these expectations are fulfilled or contradicted. The pointers here are not 'semantic' (meaningful) but 'semiotic' (significative). Virtual typography plays with the viewer's imagination as new expectations arise and what was previously seen is reinterpreted by the viewer. By applying Iser's concept of 'the wandering viewpoint' to visual communication, we can argue that the aesthetic definition of transitional graphic patterns can be employed to produce visual-aesthetic tension that keeps the viewer's mind in suspense. The viewer constantly needs to evaluate what has happened by comparing it to his or her expectations (retention), triggering new expectations of what will happen next (protension). The transitions seen modify the viewer's expectations of what is to come and the evolving shapes make the viewer reinterpret the previous events.

'...successful communication must ultimately depend on the reader's creative activity.'
Wolfgang Iser

The constant fluctuation between future and past events occupies the viewer's mind so that he or she becomes unaware of the progression of time. Perceptual creativity, or imagination, is not triggered through the precise definition of contents, but through hints that point towards them. The recipient's mind needs to be aesthetically stimulated, through literal contents or via their visual representation, so that interplay of protensions and retentions can occur. Only through providing perceptual challenges can designers manipulate people's sense of a temporal progression and make their target audience oblivious to the amount of time passing.

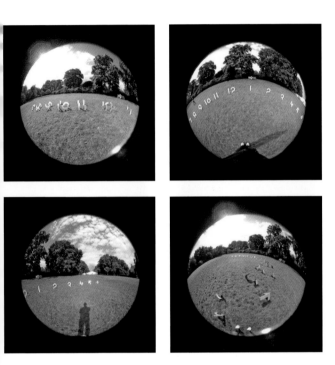

Sun Tree – Simon Husslein

> *Sun Tree* is a large-format sundial that employs the viewer's shadow to indicate the time of the day. For his outdoor installation, Simon Husslein, a German product designer, produced a series of sculptural letters and arranged them in a semi-circle. Each of the twelve abstract figures made of aluminum appears as a number when seen from one particular angle. The numbers 'one' to 'twelve' are positioned so that the viewer's shadow indicates the time by pointing towards the circle of numbers. The project was exhibited during the RCA summer show in 2007. *Sun Tree* is another intriguing example illustrating that the effective use of virtually typographical patterns does not necessarily depend on computer technology. It also reveals that outstanding design solutions can be essentially quite simple. Since graduating from the Royal College of Art in 2007, Husslein has worked as a freelance art director at s.point design in Shanghai, P.R. China, and as a tutor at Tongji University, Shanghai, P.R. China. Following his appointment as a creative director at Studio Hannes Wettstein in Zürich, Switzerland, Husslein has returned to Europe.

If we understand virtual typography as information that evolves gradually into typography instead of relating the term to virtual environments from the outset, then we may consider obscurity as one of its inherent characteristics. Typography that cannot be clearly categorised as such raises questions about its linguistic nature. The media theorist Lev Manovich describes the language of new media as a hybrid that results from the fusion of diverse media within a digital environment. Text and graphic images are used in combination with photography and time-based imagery to construct unprecedented kinds of visual aesthetics. But aesthetics can only be understood in relation to perception and we know rather little about the innovative value of multimedia typography beyond the process of production. As designers, we often assume that if media content is generated in a different fashion, and if it looks different, they will also be perceived in a different manner. But what exactly causes the viewer's mode of perception to change? And in what way are people's senses being altered?

Wirefox – Alexander Tibus
This extraordinary font was part of Alexander Tibus's degree project. Tibus has worked as a freelance designer since he graduated from the University of Applied Sciences in Berlin in 2005. Wirefox examines the relationship between text and texture. Usually, the closer you are to a piece of text, the more legible it appears. Astonishingly, Wirefox reverses this relationship. The greater the distance from which you are looking at the opposite page, the clearer the text will appear. Wirefox comes in two variations. Wirefox-Up uses an ascending line pattern, Wirefox-Down a pattern of falling diagonals. Tibus designed this font with great attention to detail. He corrected the length and width of strokes in some areas to even out the visual appearance of letters.

As it mediates the written word, typography may be considered to be a medium in its own right. At the same time typography requires other media to be delivered. Media always contain other media and at the outset we have words that reflect people's inner thoughts. When writing we translate words into **codes** following the rules given by the language system in which we choose to express ourselves. Such linguistic rules can be seen as formulae, without which written information can neither be created nor understood. Typographic information consists of letters or digits, which remain meaningless data when seen individually. Only by structuring information in accordance with the applicable formula can meaning be transported successfully. If we simplify the scenario radically we could imagine the message to be like a room, and the code a lock that prevents access. The key is like the formula that provides access to the room. If the lock is changed, the key needs to be changed as well.

'...the "content" of any medium is another medium.'
Marshall McLuhan

Codes

We have to bear in mind that the terms 'information' and 'meaning' are by no means interchangeable. Information appears only meaningful to those who understand the formula(e) involved. The understanding of a formula rests in the knowledge of a coding structure. Codes are combinations of information units, the orderly structure of which carries meaning.

Signals, signs and systems

Meaning can be built around existing signals (or data) that do not derive from human thought. Stars, for example, do not carry any meaning. But meaning can be attributed to their correlative position, as well as their apparent motion over time. Once a system had been established to determine constellations (signs), stars provided vital information about the location of a ship at sea at night. Such systematic analysis of signals follows a formula that describes the relationship between its components (information units). By defining the constellations of stars, meaning is attributed to patterns

Media

Of course, people often say they watch television rather than watch a film or the news. They listen to the radio rather than to the music on air. But this is due to the fact that people have become oblivious to the true nature of information. The confusion between the media and the message is, in other words, the result of people's misconception.

'Disorder does not necessarily mean randomness or chaos, only that it is not perceived or not perceivable as order.'
Anthony Wilden

of lights that would otherwise appear as random. The difficulty relating to multimedia communication is to separate significant codes (information) from random signals. A lot of information escapes people's perception because there is not enough time for them to assess the nature of disorderly structures. If this is the case, information remains random data – in other words, meaningless.

Message and the meaning

Contrary to Marshall McLuhan's claim, the medium is not identical to the message. Meaning, or the message, lives exclusively in people's minds. Information transmitted via media consists of nothing but codes, which need to be reassembled and analysed at the other end. However, information often changes shape when carried from one medium into another – from print to screen, for example, or from a moving image into a sequence of still ones. Information that undergoes such a transformation is trans-coded. This is part of the reason why communication often fails. If information is trans-coded, the formula needs to decode the message changes too. The definition of information that derives from the relationship between code and formula depends on the *modus operandi* of the **media** involved. This is what makes multimedia communication so complex.

In the context of virtual typography, a typographic code reveals itself gradually, as typography emerges from an abstract and potentially random graphic pattern. This means that the typographic nature of information initially remains hidden. The gradual reduction in disorder is slowed down to such a degree that the recognition process happens progressively. Depending on the amount of time delay and on the viewer's readiness to commit him or herself to the perceptual process, this can lead to either the viewer's frustration or to a sense of aesthetic pleasure. Contemporary media, such as television, often confronts people with information faster than they can decode it. The struggle for immediacy of information transmission defies the possibility of aesthetic perception. With virtual typography, the process of transition can be paced to engage the viewer more intensively in the communication process.

A code, such as a typographic message, that does not clearly expose itself right away, constitutes ambiguous information. Semir Zeki, one of Britain's leading neurologists, claims that 'we are only conscious of one of the interpretations at any given time', even if several interpretations are possible. This can be experienced when looking at ambiguous images, the visual impressions of which flip constantly between two possible states. The kind of ambiguity that is inherent in virtual typography is, however, fundamentally different. As the level of ambiguity changes over time, the guessing process is future-orientated. The question 'What is it?' is replaced by 'What will it be?' This is why the perception of virtual typography requires a progressive interplay of recognition and interpretation, which lends virtual typography its intriguing quality.

Structural decoding

Despite the fact that typographic elements become an increasingly integral part of images and moving images, the structural decoding of text remains fundamentally different from that of images. As long as people in the Western world are conditioned to write from left to right and from top to bottom, text will always be scanned accordingly. Changing the formal aesthetic representation of text will not change the fundamental characteristics of reading. However, the challenge of searching for type within moving images appears to become increasingly common.

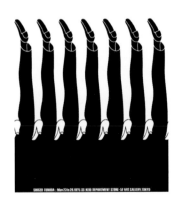

Keio Department Store poster – Shigeo Fukuda

The Japanese designer Shigeo Fukuda is a master of visual deception. As a designer and a sculptor Fukuda introduced illusionism to visual communication. Alongside dignity and beauty, Fukuda considers absurdity to be the most important aspect in the context of design. Visual challenges have become one of Fukuda's main communication principles. The poster shown here illustrates the fact that visual ambiguity offers two or more possible interpretations, but the viewer can only think of one state at a time: One sees either female or male legs.

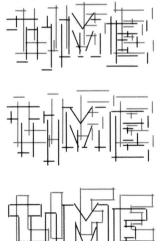

Window display – Pentagram

Time-Life, a book, music and video marketing company, have had their own building on the corner of Bond and Conduit Streets in London since the early 1950s. In 1984, the company commissioned Pentagram Design to develop a scheme for the windows facing Conduit Street. Alan Fletcher, one of Pentagram's founding partners, designed a display that revealed the words 'Time' and 'Life' only when viewed from a certain point on the opposite side of the road. Each letter was constructed from independently suspended chrome and brass rods that hung, seemingly unrelated, in space. The passer-by had to search for the correct position to decipher the text. At night the display was illuminated to provide a twinkle in the street. This project is yet another example showing that the potential of virtually typographical information was known long before the introduction of computer technology.

The Future of Croydon exhibition – Studio for Virtual Typography
In 2004 the London Borough of Croydon in south-east
England commissioned the Studio for Virtual Typography
to develop a design solution to raise awareness of Croydon's
ambitious development plans. The Studio for Virtual
Typography created a three-dimensional house-style font
(which was later named Wireframe) in order to give Croydon's
residents and visitors a sense of unity and identity. This new
typeface led to the design of a series of typographic
sculptures to be spread throughout the town. Even though
they were never produced, the designs were exhibited to
the local community as part of 'The Future of Croydon'
exhibition. The ambiguous and intriguing appearance
of the typographic sculptures was meant to disrupt people's
restless flow of daily activities and to persuade them to
explore the typographic objects from different angles.
But rather than providing time for aesthetic contemplation,
the typographic sculptures would probably have increased
the existing stress and emotional tension caused by
the town's confusing architectural environment. Busy
environments do not always lend themselves to the
implementation of virtual typography.

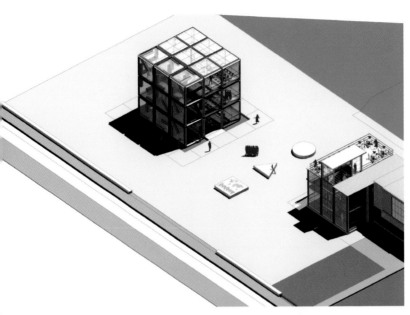

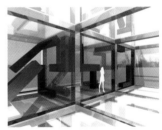

Updating modernism – Zlatko Haban and Matthias Hillner
In 2006 the Bauhaus Dessau Foundation invited architects and designers to submit ideas for redevelopment of the existing Bauhaus school (Gropius House) site. Architect Zlatko Haban and Matthias Hillner joined forces in order to produce the design of an exhibition pavilion. The pavilion, a tribute to the original building, was designed around the structure of the word 'modernism' in Hillner's Cubico font. Depending on the viewing angle the word would be more or less legible. Visitors would be able to enter the pavilion and walk through the letters to view the exhibits. The project was exhibited in Weimar in April 2006.

Scratched Out – Pierre di Sciullo

Pierre di Sciullo, a French designer, created this font in 1988 following an investigation into legibility. Each letter is angrily disfigured in order to motivate readers to decipher the text that is written. Di Sciullo first used the font in 1991 to express a controversial comment on the first Gulf War. The letters were meant to rebel against the message they conveyed. The text was meant to 'refuse itself'. The type appears to hide behind a pattern.

⑥ **The significance of ambiguity:** 6.2 Time-based ambiguity
6.1 The medium and the message ←—→ 6.3 Ambiguity and memory

Letters

An Audi advert for television, launched in 2005, shows how virtual typography may affect the relationship between recognition and interpretation. In the beginning, all that can be seen is a diversity of unidentifiable metallic objects flying through an urban scene. At this stage the information does not make any sense because it does not represent a plausible real-life situation. This strange scenario raises questions and heightens the viewer's level of attention. When falling on to the ground, some of the spiralling elements appear as letters for a short moment. As they bounce off, they rotate back into obscure metallic objects. Through this process, the words 'vorsprung', 'durch' and 'technik' (meaning 'progress through technology') are displayed one by one. As soon as the first word has appeared, the viewer is aware of the typographic nature of the visual elements and additional words are expected to emerge. However, one cannot determine at which point in time this will happen, so the viewer is kept in suspense. Tension is created, attention sustained. Once the last of the three words has appeared, the metal objects collapse into shape of the latest model of an Audi A6.

The construction of meaning (that is the attribution of significance to visual signals) becomes more difficult if the stimuli are transitional and abstract. The process of visual transformation allows for infinite possibilities of evolving forms. The viewer's expectations of virtual typographic forms to change into actual typographic information may prove right or wrong. The message it is going to reveal and the typographic shape that the message will take on offers many more than two options. Thus, virtual typography shares some of its ambiguous characteristics with works of art that usually allow for multiple interpretations. The extent to which design should be dissociated from art was much discussed following the introduction of digital media to graphic design. Modernists often declared postmodernists to be artists because they sought emotional expression and individualism in their work. Modernists, on the other hand, were sometimes accused of being overly rationalist and of depriving their audience of the joy that postmodernists felt should accompany the communication process. But the attribution of meaning to visual information follows more fundamental principles, which transcend such categorical differentiations. The main question we need to ask ourselves as designers is: to what extent can we challenge the perceptual capabilities of our target audience in order to attract and sustain their attention?

'...art puts to sleep our active and resistant powers and makes us responsive to suggestion.'
Henry Bergson

Art versus design

If designers seek to sustain the attention of their target audience through aesthetic stimulation, they might want to learn from the ambiguity that is inherent in works of art. It seems that the aesthetic impact of incompleteness is too much neglected (or too little understood?) in the field of graphic design. The captivating potential of visual designs is often compromised in order to optimise the communicative efficiency of information. To verify the multitude of possible interpretations, viewers must engage their subconscious. Only with the help of their intuition (their instinctive knowledge and understanding) can viewers fill the gaps which virtual typography presents during the early stages of the display.

If information provokes simultaneously diverse possible interpretations, the human brain is intensively stimulated to verify all those possibilities in search of the correct solution. According to Zeki, it is not ambiguity *per se* but the 'capacity of multiple experiences' that is aesthetically pleasing. What is virtually typographical engages the viewer intensively because of the variety of possible interpretations. Each plausible solution requires the visual information to be compared to the variety of memorised experiences. The consecutive evaluation of several possibilities requires the viewer to invest time in the process. But with the mind preoccupied with the comparison of evolving forms and previously experienced information, the amount of time passing remains unnoticed.

'One of the functions of the brain [...] is to instill meaning into this world, into the signals that it receives. Instilling meaning amounts to finding a solution. But the brain commonly finds itself in conditions where this is not easy, because it is confronted with several meanings of equal validity. Where one solution is not obviously better than the others, the only option is to allow several interpretations, all of equal validity. [...] These interpretations must all involve memory and experience.'
Semir Zeki

The fact that the correct interpretation of ambiguous forms relies on the viewer's individual horizon of experience helps us to understand why viewers who are visually trained master visual challenges more easily than others. Designers and artists will always be able to interpret virtual typography faster than people who do not work in the creative industry. The subjectivity of perception explains why so many avant-garde design solutions have failed to succeed in the context of mass communication. What the design community praised as the forefront of contemporary design has often turned out to be too much of a challenge for the target audience of the client.

Dream On – Underware

This image shows the result of a typography workshop held by the design group Underware in Lausanne in 2005. Shopping trolleys were arranged in an empty car park to give shape to the word 'dream' on a grand scale. One could argue that the lack of clarity about the exact purpose of this piece makes it a piece of art. On the other hand, the relationship between the word 'dream' and the empty shopping trolleys, which shape the word, can be easily interpreted as an ironic comment on consumerism. Or were the shopping trolleys chosen as objects merely for their translucent appearance to help the dream-like scenario? What exactly was intended remains ambiguous, but is it not precisely this inconclusiveness that keeps the viewer's mind occupied?

Growing and fading ambiguity

Virtual typography has been defined so far by a decreasing level of ambiguity. In the context of multimedia communications during the course of this book, the level of ambiguity is not restricted to its gradual reduction. It can also increase over time. One would assume that the puzzling effect of increasingly ambiguous typography would be impaired by the viewer's ability to memorise the initial display of the text. However, it appears that knowledge of the significance of text information does not reduce the confusing effect of texts that dissolve into ambiguous patterns. Scientific studies confirm that the addition of elements does not succeed in enforcing one particular interpretation once an ambiguous image has been perceived. Ambiguity always remains stable. This is why printed typography can be intriguing, providing it is visually challenging. The confusion between image and text persists even if readers manage to decipher it. This also means that typography that is increasingly ambiguous – and that which is decreasingly ambiguous – share their need for multiple interpretations. So the dissolution of typographic patterns in the context of motion graphics is equally stimulating, as is their gradual appearance. We may, therefore, attribute the term 'virtual typography' not only to the emergence of typographic shapes, but also to their gradual disappearance, provided that a moment of uncertainty is involved in the process of transformation. This stability of visual ambiguity is particularly important because it allows for the repetition of typographic transformations. We may assume that the aesthetically stimulating effect of virtual typography does not wear off if typographic transfigurations repeat periodically.

The Face – Neville Brody

Former art director of the fashion magazine *The Face*, Neville Brody (see also pages 94–95), created aesthetic tension – not by letting typographic elements emerge, but by allowing them to dissolve. In summer 1984, both the title of the magazine's 'styles' section as well as the 'contents' logo became increasingly unreadable from one issue to the next. Typography was transformed step by step into a hermetic code that remained decipherable only for those who had followed the process of graphic abstraction from the beginning. Here we can see clearly that human perception is subjective and that it depends on the context within which information is perceived. The end result of the 'contents' logo differed from the 'styles' logo, because its glyphs bore little graphical coherence. In the end the glyphs even merged into one another. The elements of the 'styles' logo, on the other hand, sustained their individual position as well as their visual coherence throughout the different stages of transition. This is why even the most unreadable version of 'styles' remained recognisable as a linguistic code despite the fact that one could no longer read it. However, the end result of the 'contents' logo transformation must have appeared as a random pattern to anyone unfamiliar with Brody's concept of typographic transformation.

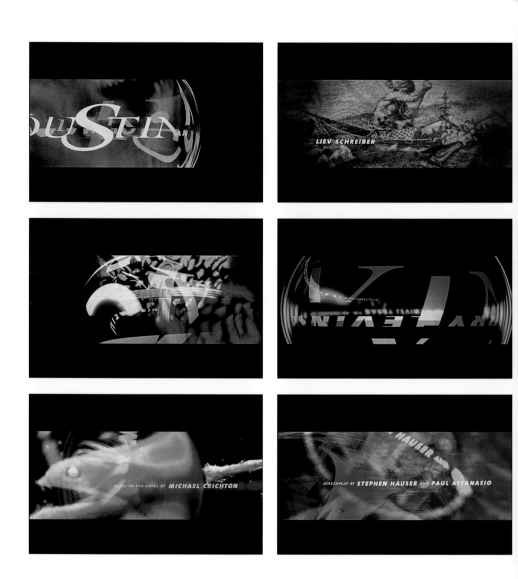

Mikon Van Gastel

Originally from Holland, Gastel moved to the States in 1995 to receive his Master of Fine Art degree from Cranbrook Academy of Art in 1997. Following his graduation, Gastel joined the multidisciplinary agency Imaginary Forces in Los Angeles. In 2000, he moved to New York to open the company's east-coast office. Gastel art directed numerous prolific projects for clients such as Nike, IBM, Motorola and Dove. In 2005 Gastel left Imaginary Forces and co-founded AVSO (A Very Small Office) in New York.

Sphere – Imaginary Forces

The title sequence for the movie *Sphere* was created by Imaginary Forces under the supervision of Creative Director Mikon Van Gastel and under the art direction of Kyle Cooper in 1998. This puzzling design solution relies on varied repetition of one particular type treatment. Words are spherically distorted so that the text elements keep disintegrating into spherical shapes as if they were observed through a transparent bubble. Despite the fact that all the distortions follow the same principle, their appearances vary depending on the way the invisible sphere moves across the text. This example of time-based typography reveals that the disappearance of type can be as equally intriguing as its gradual revelation. These variations in transition perpetuate the aesthetic tension because the viewer is led to believe that there is constantly something new to discover.

The ambition behind digital data transmission is to reduce time delays as much as possible. Real time in computational terms means to provide processing speeds that allow for the immediate availability of data. But time in real life does not necessarily mean immediacy. To improve digital communication, waiting should not be made unnecessary, rather it should be made pleasurable. Real-life experience tells us that five minutes can pass more or less quickly depending on our state of mind. The degree to which we worry about the time passing depends on our experience at present, on how it affects us emotionally. The problem in relation to digital text communication is that the acceleration of data transmission leaves no room for experiences to unfold. But communication is by definition a process. Waiting time is an important aspect in the context of communication because it allows readers to consciously select text elements and contemplate their meaning. Movement may be used to captivate people's attention, so as to reintroduce the experiential element to the communicative process and to seduce information recipients to engage with the available information. To what degree the suspension of time consciousness may intensify or weaken the reader's intellectual reflection is difficult to judge. But by turning perception into a visual challenge, the aesthetic experience provided will have a lasting impression on the reader.

*'Real time implies no waiting –
but in the real world, do we not
occasionally wait for things?'*
Jessica Helfand

Data pollution

As a result of the constant omnipresence of information
that surrounds us in digital as well as in real-life
environments, we are often too busy collecting data to
be able to select information, let alone to attribute any
meaning to it. If the elimination of time delays makes
this selection process impossible, information remains
random data. As discussed in the previous chapter,
meaning must be given to information by the information
recipient. Michael Heim, an American philosopher,
suggests a reciprocal relationship between information
density and the meaning perceived. The larger the
amount of information disclosed within a certain period
of time, the less significant it is possible to be.
Information that remained undecoded or unreflected
due to lack of time constitutes meaningless data.
Meaningless information constitutes waste, and data
pollution is the result.

The velocity of the immediate impact

Following the principles of etymology (the science of the origin of words), typography would be translated as 'writing about striking or beating', or 'a description of the mark of having been beaten or struck'. This may remind us of runes, which once were cut into wood, or of typographic stone carvings, perhaps. But in the context of screen-based communication, we could attribute a new meaning to the word typography. In the world of hypertext it is no longer the medium that is struck. The force is redirected. It strikes the reader quite directly, with the immediacy with which texts appear on screen. If the critical distance is removed it is no longer the physicality of things, but their speed, that is threatening. No longer carefully crafted, typography today is virtually thrown into people's faces when it 'pops up' on screen. When criticising new media technologies, Paul Virilio, a contemporary French philosopher, declares user-friendliness to be 'just another metaphor for the subtle enslavement of the human being to "intelligent" machines' (Virilio, 1995). If applied to typography, this statement raises questions about the efficiency-based evaluation of legible forms in the context of transitional type.

'...we drive a technology that drives our verbal life faster and faster.'
Michael Heim

The digitisation of displays

Whether or not it is beneficial to rely on virtual typography to communicate messages depends on the situation within which the information is perceived. We see printed media increasingly replaced by screens, particularly in situations where the information needs to change frequently. The check-in desks at Terminal Four at Munich Airport and Terminal Five at Heathrow Airport in London are fitted with plasma screens throughout. Even the advertising posters positioned along the elevators at various London Underground stations are now increasingly operated digitally. Initially the information here remained static. But by allowing information to move virtually from one screen to the next, and thus to follow the motion of the underground passenger, designers have managed to produce animated information that the passing viewer will find difficult to ignore. Next in line are billboards, which lend themselves to the use of digital displays.

Dromology

Dromos is the Greek word for speed. Paul Virilio coined the term 'dromology' to discuss the significance of speed in relation to the art of warfare. In ancient and modern times battles were fought to cover geographical territories as fast as possible. In postmodern societies, conflicts settle who is the fastest in covering information. Virilio describes this shift from territorial invasion to the imposition of time pressure by referring to the Cuban missile crisis in 1962. The installation of Russian rockets on Cuban territory reduced warning times between Russia and the USA from 15 minutes to 30 seconds. The so-called 'hotline', a direct telephone link between the two heads of states was put in place to avoid delays in negotiating the situation. Today we see hotlines exploited for commercial purposes. Every post-industrial market sector operates according to the first-come-first-served principle. The constant omnipresence of online information reinforces quick-sale strategies that put consumers under pressure. With its capacity to undermine this commercial battle against time, virtual typography may be considered as a kind of counter-force that seduces people to apply patience and to spend more time on information.

'"CYBERSPACE", or, more exactly, "cybernetic space-time," will emerge from the observation, popular with the press, that information is of value only if it is delivered fast; better still, that speed is information itself!'
Paul Virilio

The Source – Greyworld

In 1994 Andrew Shoben founded the artist group Greyworld, which created a digitally operated sculpture called *The Source*. The 32-metre-high installation was unveiled at the London Stock Exchange in 2004. It communicates messages that rise from a cubic constellation of 729 white glass spheres, each of which contain their own computer-driven motor, which allows it to move independently up and down along two of a total of 162 suspended strings. Thus the spheres can move into positions where they dynamically shape signs or words, illuminated in different colours, allowing for additional signs to emerge within the constellation of spheres. *The Source* provides an aesthetic response to the daily activities of international markets. Following the analysis of online data, it can display daily trading results by moving the glass spheres into the shape of arrows that move up or down. This shows how standard communication processes can be translated into artistic comments to encourage viewers to contemplate the information.

The following is a short summary of various previously discussed aspects of virtual type, highlighting what makes virtual typography different from conventional ways of presenting type on paper or on screens.

Virtual typography is time- and rhythm-bound

'...the rhythm and measure suspend the normal flow of our sensations and ideas by causing our attention to swing to and fro between fixed points.'
Henry Bergson

The gradual appearance of virtual typography produces a rhythm that makes words flow either harmoniously or in deliberate discord with the grammar of the language used. We can judge the quality of virtual typography according to when (timing), where (location) and how (animation) the typographic elements appear in relation to the meaning of the words conveyed. The time aspect that is inherent in virtual typography affects the way time itself is perceived by the information recipient. As virtual typography undermines the viewer's sensation of time, it restrains the information recipient from thinking analytically about the progression of time. Time appears to stand still.

Virtual typography constitutes a challenge

'Pure immediacy is not enough to generate aesthetic perception. Besides spontaneity, will and mental concentration are needed as well.'
Theodor Adorno

Virtual typography heightens the viewer's awareness of the temporal disposition of words. Thus it makes people experience reading as a process and helps viewers to reflect on the temporal characteristics of visual perception. Virtual typography does not facilitate the perception of information. Instead it raises questions about the visual perception of words. As communication is made deliberately difficult, virtual typography is exclusive to those who are willing to commit themselves to the challenge. But it is precisely the mastery of the difficulties involved in extracting meaning from aesthetic compositions – be they literal, visual, or both – that gives the viewer a sense of pleasure.

Virtual typography remains a mystery

Virtual typography has a somewhat mesmerising effect
on the viewer. The term 'mesmerising' has its roots in
the dubious medical practice of Franz Anton Mesmer,
a German doctor who lived at the turn of the eighteenth
century and who sometimes used magnets for healing
his patients. Mesmer's practice and theories inspired
the first investigations into hypnosis, a technique that
remains contentious to this day. The effect that virtual
typography has on viewers may appear similarly
questionable and this book alone may not provide all the
evidence necessary for us to fully approve of its benefits.
New perspectives on visual communication must be
found in order to unveil the mystery that surrounds
virtual typography before we may expect to understand
completely its *modus operandi*.

'...*"trance" is similar to other
everyday "entranced" states
such as when we are
daydreaming or become
absorbed in a film, a book,
or a physical activity and
lose track of time.'*
Richard L. Gregory

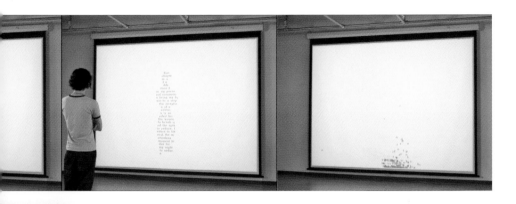

Still Standing – OBX Labs

OBX Labs is a research studio based at Concordia University in Montreal, Canada. Jason Lewis founded OBX Labs to explore new ways of integrating language with digital environments. With the help of computational artist Bruno Nadeau, Lewis produced this installation, which shows individual letters moving horizontally across the bottom of a projection screen. The random motion of letters can be disturbed by viewer interaction, a word we might want to replace here with the term 'inter-inaction'. As soon as a viewer stands in front of the screen the letters start mirroring the shape of the viewer's silhouette. But they do so only as long as the viewer remains still. Once the viewer moves, the text falls apart and the letters drop back to the bottom of the screen. In contrast to commonly known interactive media, this installation induces people to not act or interact. This behaviour of information contradicts the viewer's general experience of digital media. Instead of urging people to acquire information as quickly as possible, *Still Standing* forces the user to remain passive (not in the perceptual sense, of course). *Still Standing* can therefore be considered as a reactionary, but most appropriate, response to an increasing information density and to what Lewis and Nadeau refer to as our 'high-speed culture'.

While the viewer's mind can be captivated through visual challenges, where the viewer is not able to meet the challenge – be it due to the surrounding circumstances or due to a lack of perceptual capabilities – virtual typography fails in its purpose of decelerating the communication process. If no interpretation of the visual stimuli takes place, communication fails altogether. Therefore the perceptual challenge needs to be set at a level that is appropriate for the target audience.

Digital output

The successful use of virtual typography relies also on the viewer's focus of attention, which may be affected by surrounding distractions. However, in relation to digital communication we may assume a certain focus of attention to be conditional. Digital outputs in the context of visual communication are mostly screen-based. Even though screens take on many forms – hand-held devices, advertising displays or desktop computer systems – they are hardly ever perceived as ambient media. Screens focus people's attention and, much like a window, raise expectations of the information enclosed. Virtual typography undermines those expectations because its imperfect definition, its incompleteness, conflicts with the fundamental principles of digital systems. The concept of a digit defies any notion of transition. As opposed to analogue, digital information means simply 'yes' or 'no', 'on' or 'off', 'true' or 'false' and so on. Digital systems impose absolute measures on relative values. In their quantitative perfection, digital communication technologies do not allow for any qualitative grey zones. These grey zones, or stages of transition are precisely what we should try to reinstate when producing virtual typography.

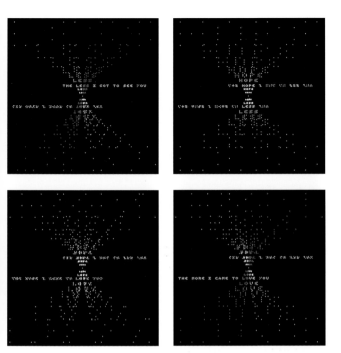

Loss of Love – Studio for Virtual Typography

This plasma screen display was inspired by Baudrillard's claim that 'Desire [...] is sustained only by want' (Baudrillard, 1990). The words 'the less I got to see you, the more I came to love you' are animated here to illustrate the idea that only that which is beyond people's reach can nourish their desires. The typographic animation reveals only one passage of the sentence at a time. As the individual letters rotate, the word 'less' transforms into the word 'hopeless' and then into 'love'. Eventually the letters rotate back to their original position and the process of transition repeats. The words 'less love' and 'hopeless' are linked visually through changes in the colour of dots as well as through the correlative position of letters. The visual presentation of these words creates a separate layer of meaning. The 'hopelessness' on the one hand contradicts the positive statement of the complete sentence. The motion of dots is decelerated to such a degree that some of them occasionally appear to be standing still. The slow, looping movement lends the graphic work a subtle quality.

The title of this final section is a Chinese proverb. Culture drives the pace of life, of which technologies are a part. In line with cultural developments in the Western world, digital technologies foster the ongoing acceleration of information transmission. But if the information density exceeds that which can be effectively acquired by the information recipient, communication fails. Unless communication processes can be decompressed, the growing information overload will continue increasingly to impair the dissemination of knowledge and understanding within society. Strategies must be found to reinstate a temporal element that is necessary for perceiving and for contemplating information.

'...the desire for the new represses duration.'
Theodor Adorno

In his opening essay in the book *Lead Between the Lines* (Haslam, 2007), Andrew Haslam, Graphic Design route leader of MA Communications at Central Saint Martin's College in London, asks: '… what does the typographic code not record? Where are the omissions?' This book tries to clarify that what type omits most and foremost is time. Conventional text presents words simultaneously. So the pace of verbal expression as we know it from spoken language is lost. Through the careful definition of perceptual challenges, virtual typography seeks to reintroduce the time factor to the communication of words.

Reading is a creative activity. Rather than passively acquiring meaning, reading is a process of actively reconstructing meaning. However, meaning is conveyed not only through texts, but potentially also through other kinds of information such as figurative and abstract image material. If textual patterns emerge gradually from imagery, the viewer's creative activity can be re-encouraged. The viewer is forced into a process of guessing the potential significance of the diverse visual elements. Where gradual changes recur over a period of time, the information recipient is challenged constantly to predict the continuation of transitions based on changes perceived in the immediate past. The rapid fluctuation of people's temporal awareness leads to the suspension of people's time consciousness and induces a sense of patience. The viewer or reader is then immersed in the perceptual experience so that temporal measures can no longer operate in a restrictive manner.

This journey through virtual type has drawn on some basics of information and communication theory, on cognitive studies as well as on various aspects of the history of typography and multimedia. However, the main argument has been built around philosophical concepts that have been established in the field of phenomenology. The gist of this book, which is admittedly hypothetical to some extent, leads away from the pragmatism that has been cultivated by designers and industries over the past decades. The principles of legibility and usability should by no means be considered obsolete. But communication must not be reduced to functional aspects alone: aesthetic perception is another essential aspect. This book may help to provide grounds for a critical assessment of functionalist principles on the basis of aesthetic concepts, and to establish phenomenology as a paradigm, not in the place of, but in addition to semiotics, semantics and pragmatism.

Bibliography

Abbott Miller, J. 1997. *Dimensional Typography: Words in Space.* New York: Princeton Architectural Press

Adorno, T. and Hullot-Kentor, R. 1998. *Aesthetic Theory.* Minneapolis: University of Minnesota Press

Ambrose, G. and Harris, P. 2006. *The Fundamentals of Typography.* Lausanne: AVA Publishing SA

Aynsley, J. 2001. *Pioneers of Modern Graphic Design, A Complete History.* London: Mitchel Beazley

Barthes, R. 1977. *Image Music Text.* London: Fontana Press

Barthes, R. 1972. *Mythologies.* London: Random House

Barthes, R. 1980. *The Pleasure of the Text.* New York: Farrar Straus Giroux

Baudrillard, J. 1988. *The Ecstasy of Communication.* New York: Semiotext(e)

Baudrillard, J. 1990. *Seduction.* New York: St Martin's Press

Bellantoni, J. and Woolman, M. 2000. *Moving Type, Digital Media Design.* Hove: RotoVision

Bellantoni, J. and Woolman, M. 2000. *Type in Motion, Innovations in Digital Graphics.* London: Thames and Hudson

Bergson, H. 2001. *Time and free will, an essay on the immediate data of consciousness.* New York: Dover Publications Inc.

Benjamin, W. 1999. *Illuminations.* London: Pimlico

Block, F., Heibach, C., Wenz, K. (eds) 2004. *The Aesthetic of Digital Poetry.* Ostfildern-Ruit: Hatje Kanz

Bohn, W. 1986. *The Aesthetics of Visual Poetry, 1914–1926.* Cambridge: Cambridge University Press

Boyarski, D. 2000. *The Poetics of Interaction, Speech* at the Oullim Design Congress in Seoul

Brody, N., Wozencroft, J. 1991–1999 *Fuse,* FontShop International, Berlin

Brown, J.W. In: Goguen, J.A. 1999. 'On Aesthetic Perception', Journal of Consciousness Studies (Volume 6)

Carson, P. 2005. *Graphic Poetry.* Hong Kong: Victionary

Crow, D. 2003. *Visible signs, an introduction to semiotics.* Lausanne: AVA Publishing SA

Crow, D. 2005. *Emblem Issue 1,* Righton Press. Manchester: Manchester Metropolitan University

Crow, D. 2006. *Left to Right.* Lausanne: AVA Publishing SA

Deleuze, G. 1989. *Cinema 2: The Time Image.* London: Continuum International Publishing Group

Deleuze, G. 2001. *Cinema 1: Movement— Image.* London: Continuum International Publishing Group

Droste, M. 1998. *Bauhaus, 1919–1933.* Cologne: Benedikt Taschen Verlag

Ellis, R.D. 1999. 'The Dance Form of the Eyes: What Cognitive Science can Learn from the Arts', in: Goguen, J.A. 1999. Journal of Consciousness Studies (Volume 6), Art and Brain, Imprint Academic, Thorverton

Enneson, P. 2005. 'Lateral Interference, Response Bias, Computation Costs and Cue Value', in: Typo, typography, graphic design, visual communication, Vydavatelství Svet tisku, Czech Republic

Fawcett-Tang, R. (ed) 2007. *New Typographic Design.* London: Lawrence King Publishing Ltd

Flusser, V. 2000. *Toward a Philosophy of Photography.* London: Reaktion Books

Friedl, F. Ott N. Stein, B. (eds) 1998. *Typo.* Cologne: Könemann Verlagsgesellschaft mbH

Goodman, N. 1976. *Languages of Art.* Indianapolis: Hackett Publishing Company Inc.

Gregory, R. 1998. *Eye and Brain.* Oxford: Oxford University Press

Gregory, R. 2004. *The Oxford Compendium of the Mind.* Oxford: Oxford University Press

Greiman, A. 1990. *Hybrid imagery: the fusion of technology and graphic design.* London: Architecture Design and Technology Press

Greiman, A. 1998. *Floating Ideas into Time and Space.* London: Thames and Hudson

Hall, E. 1990. *The Silent Language.* New York: Random House

Hannam, B. 2004. *Seeing, Thinking & Designing Three-Dimensionally,* speech at the Typo.Graphic Conference in Beirut, Lebanese American University, Beirut, Lebanon

Heidegger, M. 2006. *Sein und Zeit.* Tübingen: Max Niemeyer Verlag

Heim, M. 1987. *Electric Language.* New Haven/London: Yale University Press

Heim, M. 1993. *Metaphysics of Virtual Reality.* Oxford: Oxford University Press

Helfand, J. 2001. *Screen, Essays on Graphic Design.* New York: Princeton Architectural Press

Ikonen, T. 2003. *Moving text in avant-garde poetry. Towards a poetics of textual motion* website: <www.dichtung-digital. com/2003/2004-ikonen.htm>

Iser, W. 1978. *The Act of Reading.* Baltimore: John Hopkins University Press

Ishizaki, S. 2003. *Improvisational Design: Continuous Responsive Communication.* London: The MIT Press

Jaques, E. 1982. *The Form of Time.* Portsmouth: Heinemann Educational Books

Kandinsky, W. 1979. *Point and Line to Plane.* New York: Dover Publishing

Kemp, S. (ed) 2007. *Research rca,* Royal College of Art, London

King, E. 2005. *Robert Brownjohn, Sex and Typography.* London: Lawrence King Publishing Ltd

Kracauer, S. 1995. *The Mass Ornament, Weimar Essays.* Cambridge: Harvard University Press

Lanier, J. 1999. 'What Information is Given by a Veil?', in: Goguen, J. A. 1999. Journal of Consciousness Studies (Volume 6), Art and Brain, Imprint Academic, Thorverton

Larson, K. 2005. 'The Science of Word Recognition' in: Typo, typography, graphic design, visual communication. Prague: Vydavatelství Svet tisku

Leader, D. 2002. *Stealing the Mona Lisa, What art stops us from seeing.* London: Faber and Faber Publishing

Levinson, P. 1997. *The Soft Edge.* New York: Routledge

Levinson, P. 1999. *Digital McLuhan, a guide to the information millennium.* New York: Routledge

Lévy, P. 1998. *Qu'est-ce que le virtuel?* Paris: Éditions La Découverte

Lewis, J. 1996. *Dynamic Poetry,* MPhil Thesis, Royal College of Art, London

Lewis, J. and Nadeau B. 2005. *Inter-inactivity,* Digital Arts and Culture Conference. Copenhagen

Maeda, J. 2000. *Maeda & Media.* London: Thames and Hudson

Maeda, J. 2004. *Creative Code.* London: Thames and Hudson

Manovich, L. 2001. *The Language of New Media*. Cambridge: MIT Press

Manovich, L. 2006. *After Effects, or Velvet Revolution in Modern Culture. Part 1*

Manovich, L. 2006. *After Effects, or Velvet Revolution in Modern Culture. Part 2*

McLuhan, M. 2001. *Understanding Media: The Extensions of Man*. New York: Routledge

McLuhan, M. 2001. *The Medium is the Massage*. Berkeley: Gingko Press

Merleau-Ponty, M. 1945. *Phenomenology of Perception*. New York: Routledge

Merleau-Ponty, M. 1969. *The Visible and The Invisible*. Evanston: Northwestern University Press

Norman, D.A. 2004. *Emotional Design, Why we love (or hate) everyday things*. New York: Basic Books

Papazian, H. 2005. *'The Bouma Supremacy'*, in: Typo, typography, graphic design, visual communication. Prague: Vydavatelství Svet tisku

Paul, C. 2003. *Digital Art*. London: Thames and Hudson

Pentagram Design. 1986. *Ideas on Design*. London: Faber & Faber

Pentagram Design. 1993. *The Compendium*. London: Phaidon Press

Pentagram Design. 1999. *Pentagram Book V.* New York: Monacelli Press

Pentagram Design. 2004. *Profile: Pentagram Design*. London: Phaidon Press

Pentagram Design. 2006. *The Pentagram Papers: A collection of 36 papers*. Chronicle Books

Poynor, R. and Booth-Clibborn, E. 1991. *Typography Now, The next wave*. London: Booth-Clibborn Editions

Reich, S.S. and Cherry, C. 1979. *'A Direct Access from Graphics to Meaning'*, in: Processing of Visible Language. New York: Plenum Press

Richter, H. 1965. *DADA, art and anti-art*. London: Thames and Hudson

Sapir, E. 1955. *Language, An Introduction to the Study of Speech*. Wilmington: Harvest Press

Saussure, F. 1974. *Course in general linguistics*. London: Fontana Press

Small, D. 1996. *'Navigating Large Bodies of Text'*, IBM Systems Journal, Vol 35, Nos 3&4

Small, D. and White, T. 1998. *An Interactive Poetic Garden*, Aesthetics and Computation Group, MIT Media Lab <http://acg.media.mit.edu/projects/stream/>

Spenser, H. (ed) 1987. *'The Liberated Page, An anthology of major typographic experiments of this century'* as recorded in Typographica London: Lund Humphries

Steiner, G. 1972. *Extraterritorial*. London: Faber & Faber

Steiner, G. 1975. *After Babel, Aspects of Language & Translation*. Oxford: Oxford University Press

Swan, C. 1991. *Language and Typography*. London: Lund Humphreys

Triggs, T. 2003. *The Typographic Experiment: Radical Innovation in Contemporary Type Design*. London: Thames and Hudson

Triggs, T. (ed) 2005. *The New Typography; Visual Communication, Volume 4, Number 2*. London: Sage Publications

Tschichold, J. 1998. *The New Typography*. Los Angeles: University of California Press

VanderLans, R. and Licko, Z. 1993. *Emigre, Graphic Design into the Digital Realm*. London: Booth-Clibborn Editions

Virilio, P. 1977. *Speed and Politics, An Essay on Dromology*. New York: Semiotext(e)

Virilio, P. 1996. *The Art of the Motor*. Minneapolis: University of Minnesota Press

Wilden, A. 1987. *The Rules are No Game*. New York: Routledge

Wong, Yin Yin. 1995. *Temporal Typography*, Master's Thesis, MIT

Wozencroft, J. 1988. *The Graphic Language of Neville Brody*. London: Thames and Hudson

Wozencroft, J. 1994. *The Graphic Language of Neville Brody 2*. London: Thames and Hudson

Wozencroft, J. 2005. *'Digital Glass'*, in: limited language <www.limitedlanguage.org/discussion index.php/archive/digital-glass/>

Zeki, S. 2003. *The neurology of ambiguity* <www.sciencedirect.com>

Websites

Many of the motion graphics featured in the book as still sequences can be viewed in the research section of the author's virtual typography website <www.virtualtypography.com>.

There is also a discussion forum to which you can contribute by emailing <research@virtualtypography.com>. In addition to this you may want to visit the websites of the contributors listed below.

www.alexandertibus.de
www.averysmalloffice.com
www.bartleboglehegarty.com
www.bigfilmdesign.com
www.burodestruct.net
www.cgstudionyc.com
www.channel4.com/more4
www.channel4.com/video
www.christiaanpostma.nl
www.davidlozano.co.uk
www.davidsmall.com
www.emigre.com
www.gordonyoung.net
www.greyworld.org
www.flat33.com
www.fontsmith.com
www.haban.co.uk
www.hamishmuir.com
www.husslein.net
www.imaginaryforces.com
www.josua-reichert.de
www.katemoross.com
www.letterror.com
www.madeinspace.la
www.maedastudio.com
www.obxlabs.net
www.pentagram.com
www.prologue.com
www.quiresiste.com
www.researchstudios.com
www.rezaabedini.com
www.ruddstudio.com
www.spin.co.uk
www.stankowski06.de
www.tomato.co.uk
www.typeworkshop.com
www.whynotassociates.com

Index

This book is based on a three-year research study that I conducted at the Royal College of Art, London, with the support of Al Rees and Jon Wozencroft. But my interest in virtual typography as well as the concept behind my Studio for Virtual Typography dates back much further. I would like to thank everyone who contributed to this lengthy, and at times tiring process. Without the encouragement and extraordinary support of the people listed below I would never have been able to push the boundaries to this extent.

None of the work samples featured in this book are the result of a 'call for entries'. Instead the projects were carefully chosen over a long period of time. I am very grateful to all contributors, who made it possible to illustrate my argument and who provided their input allowing me to explain the work in this much detail.

With regards to my business development I need to thank Clare Monaghan and Paul Moody from the NFTS. Furthermore I would like to thank the Royal College of Art as well as Amersham & Wycombe College for their support, and AVA Publishing for their keen interest in my writing – it has been a great pleasure working with both Caroline Walmsley and Leafy Robinson. I would also like to thank James West of Create/Reject for being so accommodating and for addressing my suggestions and concerns. Last, but not least, I would like to dedicate this book to my daughter Aiyana Siân who inspired me to create *Loss of Love*.

Particular thanks to:
Reza Abedini, Reza Abedini Studio, Tehran, Iran
Randy Balsmeyer, Big Film Design, New York, USA
Art Beach, Chermayeff & Geismar, New York, USA
Simon Beresford-Smith, Pentagram Design, London, UK
Dr David Berry, University of Wales, Swansea; UK
Helen Bowling, Illustrator, London, UK
Marilyn Brakhage, Estate of Stan Brakhage, Victoria, Canada
Ivan Chermayeff, Chermayeff & Geismar, New York, USA
Elisa Cohen-Pardo, Amersham & Wycombe College, UK
Kyle Cooper, Prologue Films, Venice, USA
Wim Crouwel, Designer, Curator, Rotterdam, The Netherlands
David Crowley, Royal College of Art, London, UK
Nadia Danhash, Royal College of Art, London, UK
Prof. Eugen Gomringer, Institut für Konstruktive Kunst und Konkrete Poesie, Rehau, Germany
Zlatko Haban, Architect, London, UK
I-Jing He, Painter, London, UK
Simon Husslein, Creative Director, Studio Hannes Wettstein, Zurich, Switzerland
Jason Kedgley, Tomato, London, UK
Dylan Kendle, Tomato, London, UK
Dr. Emily King, Writer, Curator, London, UK
Alan Kitching, The Typography Workshop, London, UK
Jeff Knowles, Research Studios, London, UK
Alexander Lavrentiev, Professor of the Moscow University of Design, Moscow, Russia
Laszlo Lelkes, Hungarian Academy of Fine Arts, Budapest, Hungary
Jason E. Lewis, OBX Lab, Concordia University, Montreal, Quebec, Canada
Ugla Marekowa, FontShop International, Berlin, Germany
Marcus McCallion, Designer, London, UK
Susannah McDonald, Pentagram Design, New York, USA
Clare Monaghan, National Film and Television School, Beaconsfield, UK
Paul Moody, National Film and Television School, Beaconsfield, UK
Kate Moross, Illustrator, Designer, London, UK
Janet Moses, Why Not Associates, London, UK
Hamish Muir, London College of Communication, London, UK
Bruno Nadeau, OBX Lab, Concordia University, Montreal, Quebec, Canada
Zung Packer, Channel4, London, UK
Daria Polichetti, Prologue Films, Venice, USA
Al Rees, Royal College of Art, London, UK
Prof. Josua Reichert, Typographer and Printmaker, Haidholzen, Germany
Matthew Rudd, Rudd Studio, London, UK
Andrew Shoben, Greyworld, London, UK
David Small, David Small Design Firm Inc., Cambridge, USA
Godfrey Smith, Reading University, UK
Alexander Tibus, Designer, Berlin, Germany
Rudy VanderLans, Émigré Graphics, Berkeley, USA
Tomi Vollauscheck, Flat33, London, UK
John Warwicker, Tomato, London, UK
Heinz Widmer, Büro Destruct, Bern, Switzerland
Jon Wozencroft, Royal College of Art, London, UK

Photograph on page 19 by Peter Mauss/Esto
Photographs on page 21 by Carol Rosegg (left, bottom) and Richard Avedon (left, above)
Image on page 25 © DACS 2009 and courtesy of Alexander

The subject of ethics is not new, yet its consideration within the applied visual arts is perhaps not as prevalent as it might be. Our aim here is to help a new generation of students, educators and practitioners find a methodology for structuring their thoughts and reflections in this vital area. AVA Publishing hopes that these Working with ethics pages provide a platform for consideration and a flexible method for incorporating ethical concerns in the work of educators, students and professionals. Our approach consists of four parts:

The introduction is intended to be an accessible snapshot of the ethical landscape, both in terms of historical development and current dominant themes.

The framework positions ethical consideration into four areas and poses questions about the practical implications that might occur. Marking your response to each of these questions on the scale shown will allow your reactions to be further explored by comparison.

The case study sets out a real project and then poses some ethical questions for further consideration. This is a focus point for a debate rather than a critical analysis so there are no predetermined right or wrong answers.

A selection of further reading for you to consider areas of particular interest in more detail.

Ethics is a complex subject that interlaces the idea of responsibilities to society with a wide range of considerations relevant to the character and happiness of the individual. It concerns virtues of compassion, loyalty and strength, but also of confidence, imagination, humour and optimism. As introduced in ancient Greek philosophy, the fundamental ethical question is what should I do? How we might pursue a 'good' life not only raises moral concerns about the effects of our actions on others, but also personal concerns about our own integrity.

In modern times the most important and controversial questions in ethics have been the moral ones. With growing populations and improvements in mobility and communications, it is not surprising that considerations about how to structure our lives together on the planet should come to the forefront. For visual artists and communicators it should be no surprise that these considerations will enter into the creative process. Some ethical considerations are already enshrined in government laws and regulations or in professional codes of conduct. For example, plagiarism and breaches of confidentiality can be punishable offences. Legislation in various nations makes it unlawful to exclude people with disabilities from accessing information or spaces. The trade of ivory as a material has been banned in many countries. In these cases, a clear line has been drawn under what is unacceptable.

But most ethical matters remain open to debate, among experts and lay-people alike, and in the end we have to make our own choices on the basis of our own guiding principles or values. Is it more ethical to work for a charity than for a commercial company? Is it unethical to create something that others find ugly or offensive? Specific questions such as these may lead to other questions that are more abstract. For example, is it only effects on humans (and what they care about) that are important, or might effects on the natural world require attention too?

Is promoting ethical consequences justified even when it requires ethical sacrifices along the way? Must there be a single unifying theory of ethics (such as the Utilitarian thesis that the right course of action is always the one that leads to the greatest happiness of the greatest number), or might there always be many different ethical values that pull a person in various directions? As we enter into ethical debate and engage with these dilemmas on a personal and professional level, we may change our views or change our view of others. The real test though is whether, as we reflect on these matters, we change the way we act as well as the way we think. Socrates, the 'father' of philosophy, proposed that people will naturally do 'good' if they know what is right. But this point might only lead us to yet another question: how do we know what is right?

You
What are your ethical beliefs?
Central to everything you do will be your attitude to people and issues around you. For some people their ethics are an active part of the decisions they make everyday as a consumer, a voter or a working professional. Others may think about ethics very little and yet this does not automatically make them unethical. Personal beliefs, lifestyle, politics, nationality, religion, gender, class or education can all influence your ethical viewpoint. Using the scale, where would you place yourself? What do you take into account to make your decision? Compare results with your friends or colleagues.

01 02 03 04 05 06 07 08 09 10

Your client
What are your terms?
Working relationships are central to whether ethics can be embedded into a project and your conduct on a day-to-day basis is a demonstration of your professional ethics. The decision with the biggest impact is whom you choose to work with in the first place. Cigarette companies or arms traders are often-cited examples when talking about where a line might be drawn, but rarely are real situations so extreme. At what point might you turn down a project on ethical grounds and how much does the reality of having to earn a living affect your ability to choose? Using the scale, where would you place a project? How does this compare to your personal ethical level?

01 02 03 04 05 06 07 08 09 10

Your specifications
What are the impacts of your materials?
In relatively recent times we are learning that many natural materials are in short supply. At the same time we are increasingly aware that some man-made materials can have harmful, long-term effects on people or the planet. How much do you know about the materials that you use? Do you know where they come from, how far they travel and under what conditions they are obtained? When your creation is no longer needed, will it be easy and safe to recycle? Will it disappear without a trace? Are these considerations the responsibility of you or are they out of your hands? Using the scale, mark how ethical your material choices are.

01 02 03 04 05 06 07 08 09 10

Your creation
What is the purpose of your work?
Between you, your colleagues and an agreed brief, what will your creation achieve? What purpose will it have in society and will it make a positive contribution? Should your work result in more than commercial success or industry awards? Might your creation help save lives, educate, protect or inspire? Form and function are two established aspects of judging a creation, but there is little consensus on the obligations of visual artists and communicators toward society, or the role they might have in solving social or environmental problems. If you want recognition for being the creator, how responsible are you for what you create and where might that responsibility end? Using the scale, mark how ethical the purpose of your work is.

01 02 03 04 05 06 07 08 09 10

Case study: Graffiti

An aspect of typography that often raises ethical issues is the ability to make information accessible or understandable to the reader. Creative use of typography can emphasise meaning and embed emotion in words. In this way, typography becomes a gateway to verbal and visual communication, and this leads to underlying questions about the role of a piece of text.

Will it instruct, inform or helpfully guide the receiver toward something beneficial? Or might it confuse, frighten or alienate all but a select few? Does a typographer have a responsibility to always be as clear, informative and legible as possible? Or are there occasions where the decorative treatment of script is far more important than the ability to read the words? How much responsibility does the typographer have for the message as well as the way it is delivered?

'A word is not a crystal, transparent and unchanged; it is the skin of a living thought, and may vary greatly in color and content according to the circumstances and the time in which it is used.'
Oliver Wendell Holmes
(Nineteenth-century poet)

Graffiti (images or lettering scratched or marked on property) has been found in the catacombs of Rome and on the Mayan temple walls of Tikal. With messages of political rhetoric or Latin curses, graffiti found in Pompeii provided us with insights into the daily lives of people during the 1st century. As it does today, graffiti reflects the writer's views of society.

During the student protests and general strike of May 1968 (in France), revolutionary, anarchist and situationist slogans such as 'be realistic, demand the impossible' covered the walls of Paris and articulated the spirit of the time. At the same time in the US, street gangs were using graffiti as a means to mark territory. Signatures (or 'tags'), rather than slogans, were used by writers such as Top Cat and Cool Earl in Philadelphia. Cornbread, credited as the father of modern graffiti, began his career in graffiti by writing 'Cornbread loves Cynthia' all over his school. He then expanded by 'bombing' the city with his tag: 'Cornbread', written with a distinctive crown drawn over the B.

In the early 1970s, graffiti moved to New York and writers such as TAKI 183 began to add their street number to their nickname and cover subway trains with their work. Tags began to take on a calligraphic appearance in order to stand out. They also began to grow in size and include thick outlines. Bubble lettering was popular initially before 'wildstyle' – a complicated creation of interlocking letters using lots of arrows and connections – came to define the art of graffiti.

The use of graffiti as a portrayal of rebellious urban style led it into the mainstream. In 2001, Stephen Sprouse, in collaboration with Marc Jacobs, designed a limited-edition line of Louis Vuitton bags that featured graffiti scrawled over the company's monogram pattern. In 2008, Dell announced that in collaboration with Brooklyn-based artist Mike Ming, it would produce laptops with cover artwork described as 'a fluid, graffiti-inspired tattoo effect that lets style pioneers add another level of individuality to everyday life'.

Despite its rise to a recognised talent, graffiti is illegal when it is applied to property. In most countries, defacing property without permission is considered vandalism, which is punishable by law. If caught, graffiti writers can face strict penalties, including large fines and imprisonment. As vandalism, some argue that graffiti leads to increased crime and urban decay. It has also been accused of decreasing property value and contributing to business decline in some areas. Governments are spending vast sums of public money to remove graffiti. A 1995 study by the National Graffiti Information Network estimated that the cost of graffiti clean-up in the US was approximately US$8 billion annually.

If it is illegal, is it also always unethical to graffiti on someone else's property?

Are companies exploiting graffiti if they use it to sell commercial goods?

Would you be prepared to be imprisoned to communicate a message?

AIGA
Design business and ethics 2007, AIGA

Eaton, Marcia Muelder
Aesthetics and the good life 1989, Associated University Press

Ellison, David
Ethics and aesthetics in European modernist literature 2001, Cambridge University Press

Fenner, David EW (Ed.)
Ethics and the arts: an anthology 1995, Garland Reference Library of Social Science

Gini, Al (Ed.)
Case studies in business ethics 2005, Prentice Hall

McDonough, William and Braungart, Michael
'Cradle to Cradle: Remaking the Way We Make Things' 2002

Papanek, Victor
'Design for the Real World: Making to Measure' 1971

United Nations
Global Compact the Ten Principles
<www.unglobalcompact.org/AboutTheGC/TheTenPrinciples/index.html>